T0063116

TOMORROW CAN'T WAIT

TOMORROW CAN'T WAIT

An Inspirational Book Offering
Persistence for a Lifetime

Dr. Allana Todman-Da Graca

TOMORROW CAN'T WAIT
An Inspirational Book Offering Persistence for a Lifetime

iUniverse books may be ordered through booksellers or by contacting:

iUniverse
1663 Liberty Drive
Bloomington, IN 47403
www.iuniverse.com
1-800-Authors (1-800-288-4677)

ISBN: 978-1-4917-3797-2 (sc)
ISBN: 978-1-4917-3798-9 (e)

Library of Congress Control Number: 2014910832

Printed in the United States of America.

iUniverse rev. date: 11/03/2014

Also by Dr. Allana Todman-Da Graca

Tomorrow Can't Wait Podcast Series
Temple: Self-Discovery of Truth

Contents

Acknowledgments

I would like to acknowledge the individuals who encouraged and supported me while I completed this book. First and foremost, I would like to acknowledge my editor. I would like to thank Dr. Bruce Cook, who offered his depth of insight and overall encouragement. I would like to thank the Maude P. Ragsdale Library for opening their space for learning. The young ladies and women who were able to be a part of the learning process helped to structure the probing questions in this book. I would like to acknowledge the library staff for their dedication and commitment to providing learning opportunities for those who participated in this transformational journey.

I extend special thanks to all of the women who served as my mentors, advisers, and supporters through the years. I am grateful for the guidance and support they have offered through my personal, professional, and spiritual development. For all of My Girls, I express gratitude for your continued support. I would like to thank all of the influential friends and family for their continued support. I would like to thank the University of Massachusetts–Amherst and the affiliate organizations (Boundaries Crew, the Every Women Center, the Women Studies Department, and the BDIC division) for the training and exposure to innovative leadership. These experiences were crucial for my development during the formative years.

Dale Preston and Michael Lang at Gold's Gym West Cobb continue to inspire me with their commitment to helping women gain self-confidence and health with their energy and *pump-up sessions* in the gym. Thanks for reminding me to stay steady in my commitment to be the best I can be.

Ongoing gratitude is extended to Pastor John Fichtner for all of his time, patience, and energy to answer tough questions. I appreciate your council and leadership more than you know.

Thanks to my colleagues, friends, and artists for living out your lives with hard work and persistence. Any creative insight has been created from meaningful exchanges at Emerson College, Boston City Lights, Boston Center for Performing Arts, and University of Massachusetts–Amherst. Thanks to the Da-Graca clan for challenging me to think globally.

My supportive husband, Manuel, continues to support my efforts of inspiring individuals to lead purposeful lives. Thanks for providing me with the necessary patience, wisdom, and discernment for completing this book. Thanks for standing with me on this journey.

Introduction

Why Tomorrow Cannot Wait

Why can't tomorrow wait? Because many opportunities await you today.

I have written this book for people who are struggling in a stagnant place in life and yet desperately want something new. I am addressing warriors who have endured life's trials with hopes for a brighter future. There is no distinction of class for my readers. Rich or poor, anyone can experience the essence of pain.

This book is for those living between a rock and a hard place. You are a hard worker, a giver, a friend, a spouse, and a confidant. You have spent many years giving to others but feel deep dissatisfaction that stems from not telling your truth.

I thank God every day for therapists and psychologists who patiently listen. I feel great concern for thousands of people who struggle with the depression, obesity, and fatigue that emerges naturally from the battle—the daily rigor of life. Indeed, we would be lost without the patience and professionalism of counselors.

As for myself, I have also confronted significant losses. There are times when nothing seems to halt my thoughts, concerns, and subtle fears. These are the moments when there is no friend to call. My hubby may be sleeping and the gym is not open to relieve my intense stress through physical exertion.

Sadly, it's at times like these when those inner pains come to the surface, leading us to come to a valley of decision. Sometimes a bad decision leads to years of trouble.

This book helps you avoid these situations. In my case, I rely on several well-researched transformative techniques. This book is based on the assumption that individuals have a personal desire to reach their personal and professional goals. This can be measured by the level of intrinsic motivation an individual has. In good cases, this person may be self-driven and able to reach goals without a challenge. In other cases, individuals may see where they would like to be but find it difficult to ignore the negative memories, past failures, mental doubts, and practical challenges that negate the ability for them to move forward. Although we may set new goals to arrive at success, there may be external challenges that inhibit our potential for growth.

We may feel depressed because our life partner dominates us, showing no respect. *Oh well,* we think, *better the devil we know than the devil we don't.* This becomes our self-fulfilling prophecy; it happens because we think it. And, when it comes to self-concept, our personal trajectory goes down, down, down. Such are my sentiments as I sit in Starbucks, writing this first chapter. Here I am a recent doctoral graduate. I have completed the checklist, the expectations for whatever someone my age should have acquired: the backyard, two cats, accolades, a husband, and vacations to expensive places. My identity has been wrapped in the role of wife, teacher, and academic.

But sadly I have found myself … lost!

I tactfully dodged the pain of being bullied in my formative years. I planted my pain inward, denying the impact it had on my self-concept. I spent many years in counseling, trying to accept the things in life that I could not change. In many ways, I became a specialist in the well-known serenity prayer:

God, grant me the serenity to accept the things I cannot change,
The courage to change the things I can,
And the wisdom to know the difference.

Still, I felt abandoned. No matter how much I gave to myself or others, I always felt empty. Yes, I was the best person to give someone inspiration: an encouraging word or song. At the same time, when reflecting on my own personhood, I felt angry and resentful. I saw others leading their lives normally while I was a victim to a level of servitude I hadn't signed up for. In essence, I'd lost my ground, my way, and my voice.

Over time, I was able to regain the passion, energy, and strength to overcome my personal challenges. Much of the research I conducted around the persistence of individuals striving toward academic goals was applicable in the journey of personal contentment as well. I spoke with students, advisors, psychologists, and clergy. I reviewed articles pertaining to self-determination, motivation, and faith. Lastly, I facilitated a self-help motivational series to empower others to explore the hard questions pertaining to purpose, relationships, and more.

Today, I want to share the wisdom and scientific strategies that have helped me locate my voice. Please join me on this journey. You can transform your mind and life through a process of analysis and introspection. This book will be your interactive guide. You will read excerpts from my reflections, written in quiet moments. These excerpts reflect personal and professional experiences I have encountered over the years.

This book is not a book that promises to help you solve all of your problems overnight. Transformation is a process that takes time and dedication. We always marvel at the before and after photos that flash across the screen for a weight loss infomercial, but the reality is that there is a period of time between the beginning and ending of a transformation.

This book is not filled with academic jargon that may detract the reader from gaining the key concepts of self-awareness. There are a plethora of books and articles that one can find for this. This book is about the person who is often the most forgotten about after handling life responsibilities: the person who stands in front of the mirror is you. It's about taking immediate action to change the direction of your life for the better. This book is a practical guide that any reader can use to find clues to enhance his or her life.

This book will ask tough questions. I hope you will spare some time during your day to face these questions. You may want to return to the book to gain inspiration after answering the questions. I'll be here with you all the way!

I look forward to growing with you.

Allana

Live a Drastically Different Life

Sometimes we need a wake-up call. It brings clarity about where we are in life.

My life was a virtual whirlwind from 2007 to 2009. I had just left one position (drama and speech instructor) to take on a full-time position as a speech communications instructor at a college in Atlanta. My days were busy. Classes began at eight in the morning and I did not get home until ten at night. I loved my classes because they allowed me to learn about my students' lives. At the same time, I had enrolled as a doctoral student at Capella University. My days were truly intense, and I was lucky if I had even one solid meal, and even this would always be late at night. Instead, I had bagel binges during the day and feasted on Oreo cookies, brownies, canned soup, and sometimes a loaded tuna wrap with extra cheese and mayo.

Balancing work and academic life was one thing. Being a newlywed was another.

As a housewife I was learning how to make my house a home. Back when I was single, I was just another college student who ate, slept, and went wherever I wanted. But now I wanted to show my husband a special level of care and gratitude. It was so wonderful to have him in my life.

Weekends were less intense because I didn't have to work. Still, I found myself on a military schedule: get up at 5:00 a.m., cook food for Saturday and Sunday and maybe have enough leftovers for Monday, study, grade papers, and enjoy Chinese carryout.

As time went on, I noticed my face getting plump. I would pinch my cheeks. Whenever someone took my picture, I tried not to notice anything above my neck. I felt tired and lethargic, always looking forward to a holiday when I could catch up on missed sleep. I went to work with a smile and positive demeanor, but kept noticing that parts of my body were starting to bulge. Let's get to the point: I had love handles, the belly of a pregnant woman, and intense cramps during the time of Auntie Flo. Not only that, but I was only twenty-eight pounds away from the dread two hundred. My physical condition led to additional challenges.

In 2010, I landed in the hospital. They gave me a range of tests. I was terrified when the nurse mentioned a CA125 cancer test. Oh my goodness! She explained that she had to rule everything out to explain my severe pain. But I was too young for this type of test. I thought tests of this kind were given to *other* people. In spite of my feelings, I had to face surgery.

I received a diagnosis of endometriosis. This diagnosis and the pain that comes with it often leads to feelings of helplessness. The persistent nature of this hormonal imbalance I was suffering from caused menstrual cramping that was utterly unbearable.

I researched this and discovered that unresolved personal issues, financial challenges, personal burdens, and extensive stress can contribute to uterine imbalances in women. Then I realized a diet void of fruits, vegetables, and complex carbohydrates contributed to my nutritional deficiency. This was my wake-up call: a call for me to look at my health in a different light.

I began to analyze the events that had led me to this imbalanced life. I knew women who bluntly said this just happens to some people, not to others. In fact, I truly believed my inner being had a lot more information about my condition than I wanted to know. Two years after my surgery, I shifted in my bed and reminisced over losses and challenges that I had endured. I asked, "Why so much pain? Why did I cry all those tears?" I sincerely hoped someone would pop out of the sky and give me an answer.

Then I heard a still small voice. It said, "Allana, yes, you have had many challenges in life. Yes, it's been painful. Allana, what if you woke up tomorrow and lived a radically different life? How would you live? How would you be? What would your speech be like? What would happen if you only had six months to live? Would you still dwell on your troubles? Here's a plan. Do something you would never do!"

The voice was so right. I usually avoided sudden changes, but if ever I needed a change, I needed it now! So I reached out. I immediately got the idea to create a video blog of my personal stories of inner healing to other women. Of course, the blog showed my face. I discussed my weight loss challenges and efforts to become the best Allana I could be. Soon my fellow bloggers let me know I was not the only one questioning the impact of stress, poor diet, and imbalanced lifestyle choices. I even dared myself to videotape my weight loss journey. How absurd! Why would I actually videotape myself for the world? What would I say?

I woke up the very next day and created my own YouTube page. This really felt weird at first. But, as time went on, I felt a strong sense of freedom, adventure, and confidence. I thought nobody would be watching me, but the YouTube viewing statistics told me something different: I had many viewers. Many women had similar concerns. I even had awesome exchanges with women who were fighting to live healthier lives. For them, weight loss was essential just to stay alive.

Looking back, I feel proud of my decision to live a drastically different life. Facing my weight-related illnesses caused the greatest change. I lost about thirty-five pounds in nine months!

People began to ask me what I was doing. They were desperate to know how I had managed to lose so much weight. Of course, they could not see me planning out my meals, buying fresh vegetables and fruits for smoothies, or having my own personal *Biggest Loser* Challenge in the comfort of my home. All they could see was my outward appearance.

But the change really began the moment I answered the challenge to start a *drastically different life.*

Questions for Growth

A. What barriers have you noticed in your innermost thoughts?

B. Have you viewed these barriers as an excuse to hold you back from making the necessary changes in your life?

C. What is one *action* you can take today that would move you toward making a positive transformation?

D. If you have the courage today, how can you start a life that's *drastically different*?

Day Two: Tomorrow Can't Wait

Maintain Desire and Reject Desperation

At dinnertime, my hubby and I frequently discuss interesting topics. One night, we started talking about relationships. Our conversation was lively, but we had no idea we would end up taking about balance.

A relationship is a balancing act. On one hand, you risk suffocation. You love being with your partner but you want them free to grow and make life discoveries on their own. As a single woman, I was determined not to act like other married ladies. They seemed to call their husbands every fifteen minutes to see how their day was going. But eventually, I had to reevaluate my attitude. Here I was, calling hubby at least twice a day. I wanted to know how his day was, what he wanted to eat for dinner, whether he had paid a particular bill, whether we would still have our date night, and so on

On the other side of the balance sheet, I realized I needed to get busy with my own personal goals. Either of us could start feeling resentment for the other, especially if one of us tried to achieve dominance. I needed a dynamic identity to excite him and to avoid stifling his personality. Truly, men still love to chase.

As a professional who conducts seminars and workshops for women, I often field questions on the subject of marriage. Yes, many women are hoping to find a stable man who has it all together. Women desire to feel loved and feel safe with a man. Once, during a women's session, the topic of finding Mr. Right came up. Many women describe their ideal for a potential partner, and we come to the elements of loyalty and punishment. Then I will ask, "If a man cheats, whose fault is it, the woman's or the man's?" Hands fly up immediately. In some cases, I see necks turning and eyes rolling. It's as if the women have all of the answers. I continue to probe, "Would you date someone who worked in a gas station?"

Immediately, I hear female responses, "Dr. D, how much money is the man making? Is he going to college?" I also hear an adamant, "*Hell no!* He needs to be bringing in some money!" Another woman living in Section 8 housing comments, "Well I guess I would stay in Section 8 housing or find a man that can take care of me and my baby." These discussions evoke issues of trust, commitment, and motivation. In the end, the group will be divided. Some women will prefer the single life. Others will accept a man if he pays their rent and takes care of their children. I even heard one woman say she had no objection if the man she was dating had another partner on the side. She could accept him as long as he was upfront with her, even if it meant he were with someone else every other night.

What a range of opinions! Expectations go from nothing to unrelenting demands. A desire can become so strong that it manifests as desperation. We need to seek a balance. If we aren't careful, we can lose the best parts of ourselves in a sea of uncertainty. If we force something through manipulation or controlling behavior, we may miss what we truly desire.

This brings me back to my dinner conversation with hubby. My husband mentioned that his friend was annoyed because his girlfriend kept pressing for a serious commitment. In a way, the man felt sorry for her and would acquiesce. At the same time, he couldn't help but notice her loneliness, for she would leave five messages on his phone every day. In her defense, I said, "What is he saying that makes her feel this way?" As we continued talking, we realized that the girlfriend was giving more time, effort, and emotional energy than his friend. I asked my husband, "Where do you think that relationship will go?" My husband said he was not sure. The male was not chasing this female; she was doing more of the chasing. Thus the man could relax and contribute very little to the match. In essence, she was falling in love with the image of *love* that she wanted this man to display—not the man.

Droves of women can relate to this scenario. I mentioned to hubby that the unfairness stems from the man's high level of interest in a woman when they first meet. He commented, "A man needs a pause! We are not like women. They want to be around us for twenty-four hours straight. But we need a break!" This clicked for me.

As women, we have to be aware of our desires. At the same time, we must be bold, keeping some aspect of mystery to ourselves. Creating realistic expectations about how we would like to be treated, cared for, and acknowledged is essential to the level of contentment we feel in our relationships. In retrospect, we can see that clear boundaries are to protect our souls from dejection and disappointment. Indeed, when my hubby and I first met, he wondered whether I would ever give him a cue to let him know he was a potential suitor, and that's what intrigued him in the first place.

As women, we can still be true to ourselves while managing a successful relationship. We can speak and live our truths by being honest about what we can do to make our lives better.

Questions for Growth:

A. How can you relate to this example of desperation?
B. What integral parts of yourself have you sacrificed in desperation?
C. Are you in a relationship? Are you still able to maintain a mystery about your personhood?

Day Three: Tomorrow Can't Wait

Pull Up Thorns
from Childhood

How did your self-view develop? Sometimes I ask my students to discuss this. I ask them to remember when someone or something influenced the way they viewed themselves. Later, reading the assignments, I encounter a plethora of scenarios. For example, many students are keenly aware of a loved one who neglected them or provided levels of disdain. Interestingly, those impacted negatively by peers or loved ones tend to comment that their own behaviors were caused by these experiences.

Once, while evaluating this particular assignment, I realized I had never really stopped to analyze how my own childhood had impacted me. Upon reflection, I realized that bullying was a part of much of my school-age experience. My first experience with bullying occurred during a bus ride on the first day of school. That day in particular can be quite scary for any six-year-old. After the bullying, I got on the bus and scrambled as fast as I could to my assigned seat. I slid over close to the window. I believe I took my pinky finger and slid it into my nostril. This was crazy, but it was my area of safety. I felt comforted by this. Unfortunately, the pinky slide out of my nose was detrimental. A long trail of snot emerged, and suddenly it seemed as if everyone on the bus had seen this. Immediately, one person yelled, "Ewwwwww the Boogy Girl." That first day became my naming session, because everyone started calling me the Boogy Girl. To make matters worse, one popular song of the day was "Get Down Boogie Oogie Oogie" by A Taste of Honey. So the kids started taunting me by yelling, "Get down, Boogy Girl." I hated it. I numbed myself up every morning just to get through the first part of the day.

Later, in sixth grade, the now-despised Jheri curl was the latest hairstyle. But, unless your hair was naturally soft, it took a lot of Oil Sheen to keep this style moist. With this in mind, I wanted my Jheri to be perfect. Sadly, on one particular day I did not have enough sheen and I would soon pay the price on the bus ride to school.

I was attending a special school program that bussed inner city kids to better-resourced schools in the suburbs. Our ride to school took about an hour and a half. There was automatic pressure to look your best and portray the best image possible. Since both middle and high school students rode the bus, the older kids tended to sit in back. This particular day, I got on the bus and became the target of one of the bullies in the back. He began to say, "Look at you, you are so black and ugly. Your hair is so nappy!" My stomach turned at each remark he yelled in front of the others. No one said anything to stop this. I cried so intently that the imprint of my face and curls was etched on the green seat cushion as we drove to school.

Again, I numbed myself after this and just accepted that I was not the prettiest girl in the world. I wrote in my personal journal that "I felt like a black marker on a black board." I truly felt invisible. Overall, my identity and self-awareness had been influenced by how my peers viewed me.

Similarly, as a young student, I internalized the messages about beauty I received from my peers, media, advertisements, stereotypes, and more. I assumed there was something unacceptable about me. There was no one in my immediate sphere to discount these messages, so I felt that my perceptions were correct. It was only after enrolling at the University of Massachusetts–Amherst that my knowledge about identity would come to my rescue.

While at U. of Mass., I headed to the eleventh floor of the library. I immersed myself in articles from many places around the world. I wanted to understand why *I* was such a problem. Why did I have to endure the years of name-calling and bullying regarding my outward appearance? It truly baffled me. Why did the words of people matter so much? Could I find information to prove these messages were false? I began to read historical articles about the descendants of African-Americans. I also read about the lineage of kings and queens who looked the same way I did. This was monumental. I realized that some of the messages I had internalized came from ignorant individuals who were not privy to the vast world we live in. I felt a sense of indignation and resolved from that moment to teach other women to love everything about themselves.

My life took a radical turn. In essence, I was able to let go of the bullying that had initially numbed my emotions. This learning experience was a redeeming moment for me, and I was able to change the course of my life decisions.

I recently conducted a workshop at a library used by middle school girls. It was a small open area. I had these girls discuss distractions they encounter when going to school. As I was speaking, I noticed two young people who were doing searches on the library computers. During one portion of the discussion, I explained that peer pressure and bullying are most likely to occur at school and at home. When I said this, the girls at the computers slowly turned toward the workshop I was leading and eventually tuned in to the entire discussion. I wrapped up the workshop, offering tips on how girls could maintain their authentic selves as they grow into young women.

Afterward, the two girls ran up to me, and one of them asked, "Who are you?" She continued, "Everything you are saying is true. I am much older than these girls but I am going through all of this right now."

She had endured years of bullying. She said, "I have to find a way to keep this from getting to me as much as it does. When someone says something to me or calls me names, I just lose it. When I was on the bus going to school, one of the boys called me fat, and I was so mad that I jumped over two bus seats and hit him in the head with a bottle. It was really bad." The young lady eventually got suspended from school and lost the opportunity to engage with her peers. She explained that she wasn't able to control her temper. Meeting this young lady caught me by surprise.

Another girl, who was only in the seventh grade, walked toward me with her head down. She said she hated her face. When I told her she was beautiful, she said, "But I wear glasses."

Taken together, these experiences show how important it is to face the personal demons that can stunt our growth. For these ladies in the midst of adolescence, understanding their value and self-worth was crucial. In essence, it is important to unveil the hurts in our lives but then reach back and help those who remind us of the problems we faced back then.

Negative perceptions can be detrimental if not addressed head-on. All the events I have described took place outside of classroom walls. Thus, the choices and decisions were made from a personal mind-set. We cannot expect teachers and our loved ones to always understand the weight of negative actions toward us. Perhaps these individuals have not addressed their own closet of childhood pain. We can begin by using these experiences to address areas of our personal lives in which we want to grow. We can find strategic steps to help us emerge victoriously from the box created by negative experiences.

Questions for Growth:

A. What are your three strongest memories of pain as a child?
B. What emotions come to surface as you recall these memories?
C. How have these experiences impacted your choices in life?

These Goals Are *Yours*— Don't Press Delete!

Once, I was invited to speak in a panel discussion for adult learners. We were analyzing the challenges of pursuing a doctorate degree. All panelists had to face probing questions. For me, the most memorable was, "In your studies, what was your darkest moment?"

For my darkest moment, I recalled forming the first chapter of my doctoral dissertation. The whole idea of writing a dissertation was so new. I did have an idea. Since I was working at a community college, I was interested in the school's retention problem. So I started writing down thoughts on learner's persistence. Eighty pages and nearly a year later, I showed the result to my academic mentor. She was perplexed. Finally, she suggested I start again from scratch.

Here I was in my first year of a doctoral program and I was still at chapter one! There were no headlights to lead me forward in my academic progression. I was so upset. This situation got me worrying, and soon I analyzed my academic plan. I realized it would be at least a year and a half more before I could graduate. I was baffled. I had no problem dealing with academic studies, but now my research was taking a direction of its own. I painfully deleted my eighty pages and started from scratch. It was so difficult to start the process again. Fortunately, I discovered a better approach. That was nice, but I was still worried. After all of the tears, I realized that time was of the essence. I would only waste more time if I continued grousing about the year I had wasted.

While I had strong differences with my advisor, I can still hear her words: "Don't spend your time crying over this situation. Use this energy to be more productive!" This was stern but true. First, I realized that I would have to own up to my expectations and grapple with more effective learning mechanisms. I readjusted my expectations and adopted a more realistic view of my personal goals. Second, I pulled out a daily planner and began to set realistic goals that included more time for unexpected research challenges. Last, I observed the aspects of learning that were important to me. For example, I switched to a mentor who could better help me become more productive and efficient. Finally, after four and a half years, my research came to fruition. Thanks be to God, my dissertation was approved!

I described this experience to the audience at the panel discussion. Then, surprisingly, one of the doctoral students posed this question: "I have already conducted doctoral work at a prior institution. I had a situation that was similar to what you spoke of about deleting a lot of research that was already conducted. I am just unsure if I can really do this because I want to be successful. Do you have any advice or suggestions for me?"

I knew I was in the right place when she posed this question. It seemed like yesterday when I had been in the same shoes. I commented, "There's a reason why you showed up today. There's a reason you reenrolled despite your negative experience. Your research has a purpose. Can you accomplish this purpose if you ignore criticism? Think of the voices that will not be heard if you do not use your interests to find these answers. You are the best person to say, 'I can't delete my plans because this person will not get my help if I do not persist.'"

In essence, there are many life challenges that make us question our ability to be successful. We must maintain resolve, heeding the inner voice that gives us momentum to work in our field. We cannot be afraid to revisit our goals in an effort to be more effective. This may mean looking at our sphere of influence and finding the individuals who are the greatest and least influential.

As an analogy, think of the weeding process when you are grooming a garden. Too many thorns can choke budding plants. In the same way, you have a responsibility to cultivate the goals and passions in your life. Your purpose in life is rich and full of possibilities. Continue to thrive by discovering ways to allow your goals to blossom. Do not press delete on your goals!

Questions for Growth:

A. What is one goal you presently have?
B. Have you had moments of doubt or fear?
C. What are the messages you internalized as a result of these moments?
D. Why do you feel this way?

Day Five: Tomorrow Can't Wait

Unique Fingerprints, Unique Purpose

I want to encourage you. Step out and do whatever you've wanted to do for years. You're never too old to do what's deep within your heart. Do you fear that others will hate you for doing this? Remember, your enemies are only there to make you stronger. Often, they hate because, unlike you, they lack the gumption to step ahead on their own. Discretion is the key to reaching deep within your soul. I believe that every person has a time in life where they seek to fulfill a new goal or purpose. I encourage you to take a small step in that direction. Give your passion in life room to develop today.

For example, I used to tell people that I wanted to encourage and uplift women through art and writing books. Many of my skeptics said, "How will you make money with that?" Others said, "You'll be sitting around and worrying about paying your bills!" I let these comments thwart my desires for five years.

What a waste of time! I allowed negative ideas to make me skeptical of the innate vision that God had given me. Instead, I pursued get-rich-quick schemes and listened to half-baked truths about how to succeed. Eventually, I came full circle. I recognized that no one could truly understand the fire that was deep within me. I realized that I didn't have to be Oprah, Dr. Phil, Iyanla Vanzant, Anthony Robbins, Les Brown, Joyce Meyer, or any other familiar name, because the fingerprints God designed for me were unique. I realized that I had a specific purpose that was distinctly mine.

I believe this about everyone. I remember a story about a preacher. He talked about someone who had purchased a first class airplane ticket but was mistakenly seated in economy class. The passenger complained to the flight attendants. He stressed how important he was and demanded to be placed in first class. Finally, the flight attendant moved the passenger and the plane took off. As soon as the plane was in midflight, the pilot said, "We should be landing in Miami shortly."

The passenger protested, "Miami! I am heading to New York City!" The preacher concluded by commenting that, in life, there are many people on a first class trip to a wrong destination!

I experienced a profound change when I tuned out the haters, doubters, and misleading individuals I had feared. I started to affirm that there was something unique and special about myself. Soon I felt so moved by this that I wanted to help other women feel the same joy. The results were amazing. When I recited a poem or sang at a poetry or seminar presentation, women told me how I had uplifted and inspired them. I'll never forget one woman's letter about how a simple hug from me had prevented her from committing suicide.

Love is priceless. We women are truly blessed. We are mothers, daughters, friends, and nurturers. In my case, I have been blessed to share what's on the inside. I am confident that you can do the same. This statement sounds easier than it is to practice. We cannot extend what we don't have to give. Taking moments to learn about our inner traits, strengths, and weaknesses can afford us the ability to have compassion and appreciation for others. Look to receive affirmation and encouragement from communities and organizations that align with your values and views. When we do this, we are able to take the focus off of ourselves with the intent of finding a way to help someone else. This gives us the ability to not only give love but to receive that which we so desperately long for.

Yes, I have already taken a number of wrong flights. Have you? It doesn't matter now. I know you and I can make a commitment to be where we are supposed to be in our lives!

Questions for Growth:

A. Have you allowed individuals to be a poor influence on you?

B. Who would you describe as your *haters*?

C. What are some ways you can discount the negative comments from others?

D. What is one community group or organization that you can join to help you develop the engagement of love that is positive for support?

Day Six: Tomorrow Can't Wait

Love = Time

One Valentine's Day, I reflected on the ups and downs of my life. I thought about pains that deeply wounded me. Initially, I thought of negative statements I had heard from friends—things like, "You are not beautiful, you are not smart, and your hair is ugly." These hurts had become self-fulfilling prophecies for me. As a result, I never felt like I belonged. In my shortsighted view, I had internalized these comments. I hated to look in the mirror. All I could see were things that seemed strikingly wrong.

As a young teen, I did not match the images that media and society portrayed: fancy clothes, perfect hair, and an accepted caramel complexion. With a Caribbean heritage, I did not have the praised island look: a pecan tone and curly locks of beauty. I felt faulty in the way that I looked. Worse yet, peer pressure to fit in had made things even worse, and I had begun to look for acceptance from others. In adolescence, the perception of others is a nonacademic variable that poses a large threat to the cognition of a growing learner. In my introspection, I realized how much the views of others influenced my self-perception.

As I continued pondering these things, I began to ask myself, "What got you through those years? Who were the people who helped you?" Happily, I felt warm floods of emotion as I thought about the teachers I liked most. These were truly my heroes. I remembered Ms.

Ravich, my fifth grade teacher, who always had our class doing creative projects. She always smiled so nicely at us when we walked down the hall. She treated everyone with kindness and fairness. I remembered my music teacher, Ms. Maccini, and her ability to pull out my musical abilities with competitions, etc. I remembered Ms. Connolly and Ms. Dennis, who provided encouragement and recognized the public speaking skills they thought I possessed. Most important, though, I remembered my Lord of the Dance, Duggan Hill.

I met Duggan Hill because my best friend Zakyia mentioned she had an opportunity to dance as an opening act for Ray Charles. I could not believe this. How did she have this awesome opportunity? How could I get involved? She invited me to a rehearsal where an instructor would be teaching the art form of dance I loved so much. It was a lot to take in. I showed up, and it was amazing. It was near downtown Boston at a place called Boston City Lights, home for a performing arts troupe. There, I found a sea of people in front of mirrors. They were doing an original dance piece to "Rhythm Nation" by Janet Jackson. I saw the team executing drill turns and spotting in front of the mirror. I went to the back of the class, trying to hide and not be seen.

All of a sudden, I heard Duggan say, "Please come up to the front." I was extremely nervous since this was my first day. I was looking for an African American dance teacher, and this man was white with a silver ponytail. After the initial shock of seeing a white man who could dance so well, I moved to the front of the class. From that point on, he became my hero.

I attended all of the rehearsals and sometimes would show up every day of the week. I remember the first performance. He allowed me to sing Whitney Houston's "I Will Always Love You" as an opening act in a production, and had me lead vocal warm-ups before major performances. I was so nervous. My hands were clammy, my throat tight, and I felt like I had to gasp for air before my opening song. It was truly nerve-wracking. Despite my nerves and sweaty palms, I knew that Duggan believed in me. Having his faith in my abilities pushed me to believe that I could do it. I *could* execute my gift for the world. I was *worth* more than I had given myself credit for. My involvement in this extracurricular activity became important for my learning. I had a piqued desire to go to school, because my expectations and experiences of life had shifted dramatically. I was able to apply the disciplines of hard work in my academics as well. I stayed committed to the dance troupe well after high school and am still a very strong supporter.

Those formative years reshaped my self-perception in more ways than one. Duggan made a true difference in my life. In fact, my experience with the Boston City Lights team was a catalyst for a journey of new experiences. I gained dignity, self-worth, and a sense of responsibility, and I began to realize that there really were sincere people in the world. Most important, these individuals were my favorites because they simply donated their time in an authentic manner. Their service did not come with a price. Those teachers inspired me to take on the vocation of teaching in an effort to pass on the lessons they had taught me.

Questions for Growth:

A. Who are your heroes?
B. Have you ever let these individuals know how valuable they have been in your life?
C. How can you demonstrate their example in your daily life?

There Is Work for You to Do

What a beautiful sight! Twenty-three African American students were seated in front of me. But sadly, I had another class coming up, plus a pile of administrative work. I sighed, thinking of the extensive workload that lay ahead. First I noticed that David, a free-spirited and passionate nineteen-year-old, was not his usual boisterous self. On a normal day, speech preparation included multiple elocution and diction activities that most students would avoid. Yet David would tackle every syllable during the activities and command attention in the classroom.

Since this was the day for students to pick their speech topics, I began to explain the themes they could choose from (diabetes, obesity, career skills, HIV, education, etc.). I found myself wondering, *Do they really care about these issues? I do not want them to see a boring teacher reading a list of issues they cannot relate to.*

On this particular day, David refused to join our discussion on the list of topics. As I wrapped up class, I stated, "These topics are serious. Remember, you are researching themes that will have an impact on your peers."

Just then, David shot his hand in the air and yelled, "Mrs. D, I have to tell you something!" I looked at the clock. Only fifteen minutes remained before my next class and I had preparations to do. But David looked at me and said, "I have one of the problems you discussed today."

I assumed that he was referring to personal issues with time management or career specific challenges. I never imagined it would be what he revealed.

He continued, "The reason I have been acting so weird is because I have HIV. I can deal with it now, but when I first found out, I panicked and did not tell anyone, including my mother, for the first year. Finally, I had to tell her because I got extremely sick and could not get out of the bed. Once she found out, things got better because I was able to get the medication I needed."

I felt at a loss for words. I thought to myself, *What can I say that might encourage him and let him know there is still hope?* Determined, I looked into David's eyes and said, "David, no matter what, I want you to know that you still have a future! There is work for you to do in this world!" Unexpectedly, something majestic entered our conversation. I saw water build up in David's eyes as if he had been waiting to receive this inspiration for some time. I held back my tears and exchanged them for affirmative words of consolation.

David reminded me how important it is to be authentic. This discussion could have taken place anywhere. We are faced with larger challenges in our society. I can imagine the fear he felt when it came time to share, but I am reassured because he felt safe enough to pour his heart out.

I asked David if there was something I could do to spread awareness. He discussed his concern about the impact of HIV in the African American community. In addition to this, individuals with the disease suffer from feelings of guilt and shame. I closed the conversation by affirming his request to tell others about this disease. The next class bustled in as we wrapped up our conversation. I have not instructed the same since.

We may not have an HIV diagnosis, but we all have some area in our lives that nudges at our thoughts of wellness. We may be battling addiction. With every challenge, there is the possibility of regression. Any form of life challenge that follows the experience of abuse, addiction, tragedy, or loss can create spiraling patterns that lead to deep levels of fear and depression. This is the challenge for individuals.

When we let our deepest secrets out to someone close, that is only the beginning. We also have to be very careful as to how and with whom we share these experiences. Unfortunately, sharing detailed experiences about past pain with the wrong people can trigger the person with the emotions associated with the initial hurt.

This student dared to share something about his personal health with me out of a desire to receive an encouraging word. Don't we feel better when we share something that caused harm to us? When we share with the right individuals, we are able to receive the love and compassion that comes from deep levels of empathy. If you have been abused or ill-treated, consider talking to a counselor or clergy member for additional guidance. You do not want to deal with all of your challenges alone in a dark room.

Consider telling your truth in a journal reflection activity, starting with these questions. Try to make yourself accountable by telling your truth without compromise. Hopefully, you will find that this frees you from feeling the levels of disdain that come from years of held resentment.

Questions for Growth:

A. What is your biggest secret?
B. How has this secret impacted your life?
C. Write an anonymous letter to yourself in a journal. Take time to reveal your largest challenges.
D. Consider finding a counselor, close friend, or clergy member to talk to about your concerns. Write about how this makes you feel.

Day Eight: Tomorrow Can't Wait

The Weeding Process

Whenever spring arrives, I feel excited about my garden. I think of blooming roses and foliage on trees. However, I'm not nearly as excited about the weeding process. When seasons shift from summer to winter, we watch leaves falling and colors changing. We see naked trees and lifeless rosebushes. Yet we know the cold season is but a time of incubation and seed production for these plants. When spring arrives, I pull up old weeds that choke the blooming of rose bushes and other plants.

Think of this example as an analogy for removing individuals from your circle of friends. Remove those who are not a positive influence. Sounds easy, doesn't it? Unfortunately, this may require a deliberate weeding process.

While I was a college student, knowing how to cook was a convenient skill. I was so good at this that a small group of students paid me to prepare home-cooked meals for them. But, over time, I realized that their friendship was conditional. They only wanted to hang out if I could cook their meals. My last straw was having a so-called friend call me and say, "Allana, we have not seen you in a while. My girlfriends and I have brought all of the supplies so you can cook for us."

I said, "Will I be able to eat this meal too?"

As college students, we were all broke, so they replied, "No. We only purchased enough for ourselves." That's when I realized that I needed authenticity more than money and superficial friendships.

Aside from cooking, I attended college socials with my friends, but again I discovered that, in troubled moments, these friends were nowhere to be found. When finances were tight, I was uncertain whether I could finish college, and I had no peers on campus to help me. I clearly remember the day when I stopped and reevaluated my life. I wrote a few words in my personal journal during my freshmen year.

September 24, 1995:

"I feel so lazy. I mean, I really don't feel like doing anything. I mean, I know that I am in college and everything. I know I am supposed to be serious about my studies, but I just feel like I do not have the energy. In my comparative literature class, I am already two assignments behind and I am supposed to be finished with one of these books. All of these days are just going by so quickly. I do not understand. I just don't know how to push myself to think of the importance that school has. Sometimes it can be such a burden to think about my financial situation. I need to find an avenue so I can make it through successfully. I pray God will help me to make the best decisions in my life. Sometimes I wonder if the choices I am making in my life are the right ones. How can I be 100 percent sure? Today I guess I will start living for me."

From this moment, on I relocated my thoughts about friends and purpose. I asked myself what kind of student I wanted to be. I began to look for opportunities for growth by joining organizations that would respect and honor the talents I had. I distinctly remember writing another journal entry where I vowed to clear my friends list and start completely over. I even created a ceremony for it. I turned off all of the lights and lit a candle. I stared at this candle for a long time. A sense of calm and redemption overcame me as I sat in this tiny room with my little candle. Somehow, the ambience of this darkened room with the candlelight glow reminded me that I did not need tons of friends in order to shine.

I did experience a period of loneliness. Fortunately, I was invigorated by involvement with student leadership. At U of Mass–Amherst, I was able to participate in organizations like the Every Women Center, University of Massachusetts Collegian Staff, and more. One of the strongest ways to advance in life is to find ways to serve our community. I knew a change had come when a college peer came up to me at the end of a workshop I was covering for the student paper and said, "Hey, Allana, I just want to say, I don't know what you are doing, but I can see that you have changed so much. Keep it up."

Wow! Here was someone I had never talked to before. I was shocked she even knew my name and especially that she had noticed something different about me. By this time, I was a well-known writer on campus. The student body had become aware of my articles on self -awareness and motivation. Remarkably, once I was sitting in a stall in the ladies restroom and was amazed to see an article I had written plastered on the front of the door.

When I think back on these years, I realize that it was my decision to change social spheres that allowed me to experience a transformation in my life. I detached from those who were not sincerely interested in sharing and exchanging meaningful dialogue.

Questions for Growth:

A. Are you happy with the current relationships in your life?

B. If not, write a list of the friends who have been helpful with authentic dialogue.

C. Write a list of friends who have not been so helpful.

D. How do you feel after a dialogue with them?

E. Jot down several emotions that correspond with this feeling.

F. Find an organization where you can volunteer your time.

From Stagnancy to Responsibility

Once, after reflecting on my sphere of influence, I realized how important it is to check my friendships to see if they are productive or draining. One word, *stagnant*, comes to mind. This word indicates that we are like a hamster moving in circles without a clear path. How terrible to be in a position where you do not feel you are moving ahead on a personal or professional level. I do not believe that anyone wants to live a life of mediocrity.

How can we conduct a self-evaluation? We need to realize how past experiences influence our internal estimate of our potential to attain personal and professional goals.

In my experience, I had problems when I neglected to set boundaries in my personal life. I avoided setting boundaries to avoid confrontation. As a result, my resentment and anger for not creating clear expectations gave others free reign to abuse my time, energy, and friendship. For years, I had no idea how much influence negative people had on my aspirations and life pursuits. In my formative experiences, when I mentioned my dreams to peers and mentors, I realized that I had allowed these views to come at a price.

For example, when I worked as a communications intern at a well-known firm in Washington, DC, the owner asked me what I intended to do in life. Immediately

I said, "I want to inspire people with my writing, singing, and dancing. I hope to encourage people."

Granted, I lacked the vernacular to explain how I would strategize this, so the woman replied, "How do you plan to live off of that?" As a result, between 1999 and 2003, I asked people whether they were happy in their lives. Many of them did not give an answer but offered an excuse for not using inherent gifts. Some mentioned having to work too much. They regretted their inability to find time to do what they felt they should. One person told me she wanted to become a dancer but gave up on the dream once she had her son.

Now don't get me wrong. I agree that we don't have enough time to do everything we want, so we do have to make sacrifices. I do believe, however, that if one is never able to reconnect to their inner soul, to find their passions and a way to convey this in their craft, then a sincere resentment comes. We feel disdain for those who <u>can do</u> this, and this is a particularly unfruitful result.

Many people may fail to give us the advice we so desperately need simply because they themselves have not found answers to these questions. Unfortunately, if we seek support from the wrong individuals, we can be sourly impacted by this and thwart our own future because they don't offer the validation and assistance we need.

This was true in my personal experience. I spent over ten years replaying old memories in my head, thinking of interactions with loved ones. I would wake up and reflect on this, pondering how their words and reactions failed to demonstrate love. I tried to reason with unreasonable circumstances. I said to myself, "I can take put-downs and condescending words." But, inwardly, I would cry.

Finally I realized that I alone was responsible for listening when people undermined my inherent desires. I asked myself how many more years I would dwell on negative experiences. I was harboring these emotions and becoming ever more resentful. Fortunately, I noticed my cyclical emotion. I found a quiet space and acknowledged my own responsibility for being stagnant in life. I was reminded that, despite discouragement from others, I still had innate talents. I alone could decide whether I would allow negative memories to wound me to the point of inaction. It's hard to stop resenting negative people. In my experience, letting go allowed me to give the responsibility back to those people I had anger toward. I experienced freedom once I accepted people as their authentic selves. I believe that we show people how we need to be treated by the way we respond to their words. In essence, we are showing an act of love by being authentic when we receive and give.

Questions for Growth:

A. Can you recall a specific discussion where you shared something of a personal nature with someone?

B. Did the person speak to you in an objective, nonjudgmental tone?

C. If you do not feel happy at the end of the prior question, then what are you feeling?

D. Are you still holding onto resentment from the way that this discussion influenced your self-perception?

E. Consider repeating the questions above with the experience you had with someone that was supportive and affirming. What does this discussion reveal to you about how to gauge who you share your inner most feelings with?

Day Ten: Tomorrow Can't Wait

A Letter of Truth

It's especially important to think carefully when speaking to those in leadership roles. For example, as a leader, I'm always surprised when parents boast about their child's achievements. Ironically, behind closed doors, that same child will tell me how critical, unforgiving, or mean their parent has been. Although we want to challenge young people, we also want them to know that we believe in them. Over the years, I have observed that successful students have a balanced level of support and direction from their parents. This type of consistent validation and encouragement pushes the young person forward.

I'll never forget a teen who was eavesdropping while I taught some young girls a lesson on self-acceptance. At the end of the lesson, one young lady ran up to me and said she was horrified to stare in the mirror. She believed she was unattractive and a terrible person to look at. She said she had a lot on her mind. Immediately, I offered comforting words. I asked her to write a letter to tell me about challenges that prevented her from excelling. I did not see her for a while, so I assumed she had changed her mind about joining the group. Surprisingly, she came back to me two weeks later with a piece of paper crumpled in her hand. She gave it to me and asked that I read her letter. Here's what she wrote:

Dear Doctor D:

The things that are holding me back are having a bad life, being bullied, not being happy at home, and not having freedom. Those things are holding me back because I have been bullied all of my life and I try to ignore the people that bully me but they still bully me even if I confront them or if I ignore them—they still bully me. And they also talk about me with other people. I am not happy at home because I am the only child and I do not have anyone to talk to and I can't talk to my parents because it would not be right and plus I need someone. I can talk to a teen or a person that will understand what I go through every single day. So we can talk and share. I do not talk with anyone at my school because I am afraid that if I talk to someone, they are going to tell some other people and I don't want to talk to a counselor or adult.

As I read this, I couldn't help but reflect on my own childhood. As a young girl, I would stare in the mirror and wish I looked completely different. In fact, I would stare in the mirror for hours. I would beg God to give me different traits: lighter skin, longer hair, and anything else to imitate the actors I saw on television. I didn't recognize that I was ignoring the creation that made me uniquely authentic. Somehow I allowed outside words to reign more than the inner voice that told me I was OK. Words from authority figures filled me with self-hatred. As I matured, I learned how to strategically detach from the negative words that were meant to break my spirit and self. I can't shake this memory. I always think of it when a student presents challenges that seem unrelated to their ability to complete schoolwork. I still remember my own student breakdowns and challenges while I served as an instructor at a two-year college.

While I was walking in the hall, a woman approached me with tears in her eyes and said, "Ms. D, my mother blew crack in my face and told me. 'This is your future!'" I could not believe this. Another student came up to me and said neither of his parents wanted him. He pulled out an article describing horrific abuse he had endured in the foster care system. Another student commented that no one was present to attend his high school graduation. The last student said he was determined not to let circumstances rob him of his future. Moments of sadness from these painful experiences, along with the associated memories, may thwart us from being the best person we can become. Consider the option that *you have a choice* to accept the hidden messages you received from your negative experiences.

Questions for Growth:

A. What are the things that are holding you back?

B. Who do you *believe* is responsible for this?

C. How much more can you allow this to happen in your life?

D. Make one positive statement about yourself. State this in front of a mirror until you believe it.

The Value of Time

Today I learned the value of time. It's just as essential as money and health, and too often we take it for granted. Truth be told, no one walks around saying, "I'm going to give you my precious time and I want you to squander it. It's OK for you to abuse and misuse my time." In fact, life is a free gift, full of moments that can be fruitful and reciprocated with actions and behaviors of love. Unfortunately, time can be misused by people who don't have our best interests in mind.

In what ways do we throw away this precious gift of time? Well, it's when we decide to replay negative experiences like a broken record. When we do that, we are failing to honor the value of time and the precious moments of the present. It's up to us to decide what we ought to listen to.

Once I found myself staring at a group photo of friends who were no longer in my life. I was upset. I felt like I had lost out. It was like being abandoned by something owed to me. Still I kept revisiting the image, and the more I did this, the more upset I became. It turned my whole day sour. But, when I think about it, I was the one who chose to view this picture over and over again.

What was really happening? I was revisiting details of my past relationships and coming to terms with the essence of my feelings. During my time of study, I watched the documentary *Just Melvin* about adult children who experienced sexual abuse at the hands of their father. When confronted, the father denied the abuse. It was so hard to see the long-term impact that shame from abuse had on the daughters. Two of the women ended up living in a truck with all of their possessions. This was so sad. The sisters became alcoholics. At the end of the documentary, we see a confrontation when the daughters visit their father in the hospital. One of the daughters was in such pain that she stood outside the door with tears coursing down her face. She was suffering from a large knot in the pit of her stomach. You could visibly and audibly witness this woman's pain. You wanted to console and hug her, erase her pain, but it was tragic for she had harbored it for years.

The documentary would move anyone to tears. Despite the years that had elapsed since the onset of the abuse, the victims described their turmoil as if they were still kids looking to be rescued. Even now, they were stuck in a pit and unable to break from pain. I wondered what it was, in these defining moments that influenced them not to advance to their highest potential. Whose voice was the loudest in their heads? How many days, weeks, and years had gone by while they felt isolation and shame for their father's abuse?

Some of the siblings had internalized the abuse and became abusers themselves. Others lived in squalor, cynicism, and shame. Time was taken from these little girls in such a horrible and hidden manner. I truly felt for them.

I revisited my own life, jotting down notes for the decades of my life. I highlighted the pains and chains that glued me to my past from ages ten to thirty-five. Then I dared to place three extra decades after this timeline.

Finally it came home to me. Life is truly precious. I was midway in my time line to sixty-five. I had to ask myself, "How do I want the next three decades to play out? Will I allow my disappointments to replay the same pain I used to endure? What will I do differently? Where am I still stagnant? What resources do I need to pull me out of this pit?"

Time is precious. The important thing is to have more days of reawakening and discovery than of dwelling on unproductive memories. If we hold onto the anger someone has caused us, we are giving them a victory. If we do that, we end up suffocating ourselves and not being able to receive proper treatment from others... I have never seen two fists give a hug at the same time. Just tightening the nerves and clenching our hands into fists sends a message for everyone to stay away. At most, a hurt person needs a hug and words of love.

Time is precious. Choose how to observe the pains of life and navigate through your painful moments to bring about sustained change.

Questions for Growth:

A. What are the memories you continue to revisit?
B. Why does this make you so angry?
C. What resources do you need at this time to help you out of this?
D. What support systems can you use?
E. What are two action steps you can take toward addressing this problem?

Day Twelve: Tomorrow Can't Wait

New Travels = New Discovery

I was an adjunct professor for a notable university in Massachusetts when I was sent to locations where cohorts of students had enrolled in our program. I was so excited when I would get a new assignment. This was true for every city that I visited. But there was one course in Idaho and that didn't excite me. First of all, the only time I had heard of Idaho was in reference to potatoes when I went to eat dinner at the Longhorn restaurant!

This particular weekend, I was returning to wrap up a six-week course. Upon my arrival, I was surprised to see excitement on the faces of my students. This was unusual because these adult learners were sacrificing weekends to complete their master's degree in Education. On this last day, the students were supposed to bring in items of personal value. This could be a teddy bear or a keepsake item from a dear friend or loved one.

Normally, I would have everyone place their items in the middle of the room. The whole class would walk around as though they were archeologists in a museum. Very delicately, they would pick up each item and describe it, discussing its intent. It was common for students from past cohorts to bring items that were dear, but there was nothing that would stop the students in their tracks. This class was different. I saw items like a random dog tag, a teddy bear, an old ring, and a baking tool. Picking the items up, I began my descriptions: "I see a bear that was used in someone's childhood." Someone else picked up the dog tag and mentioned, "This person brought their dog tag as a reminder of high school." One by one, the students began to explain why they had placed the items in the circle.

After the initial process of guessing the meaning each item had for the contributor, the students who owned the items were asked to speak in first person as though they were the person giving the item. First, the individual who brought the baking tool discussed the symbolism of the item and how it reminded her of her mother baking fresh bread and banana bread for the family every morning. She had tears in her eyes, and we could just smell this bread baking as she described it. The owner of the teddy bear said it was a gift from her grandfather. In moments of despair, this woman would grasp the teddy bear and feel safe. Another item was a sterling silver ring, and this represented an intimate moment for one of the students. Her father was never able to say, "I love you," but in the moment before handing her this ring, he had managed to muster up these words. The room was silent and everyone was moved. Everyone waited in anticipation to see what was so special about the dog tag. Even before its owner began to speak, tears were already streaming down her face and she was trembling. She gripped the tag.

"I want you to hold onto this," she said. "You have been my best friend for all of these years. Although we can no longer speak with each other, please hold onto this and know that I will always be there with you." It turned out that this dog tag was one of the few things that her best friend owned before dying in a car accident. Instantly, everyone in the class was moved to tears. The items we saw in the middle of the circle took on a new meaning. These items were beyond sentimental because they represented memories with close ones.

In that moment, the entire class was much more than just a community of students. Now these were human beings sharing real-life experiences. In essence, we hold dear to memories of dear ones. Tangible reminders like these bring everything back as though no time has passed.

Get in touch with positive memories from your past and share them with others you trust. Take journeys in your memory to find new discoveries in the most unlikely places. Allow your mind to walk into unfamiliar pathways for new findings. Perhaps this will provide you with new memories and associations that will serve as comfort in times of pain.

Questions for Growth:

A. What is something you would like to do but felt apprehensive about?

B. What do you envision this activity to be like?

C. Consider setting a date with a buddy for this activity. Jot down your experience. What new findings about yourself did you learn?

Step It Out Alone

It's difficult to do something alone. My lesson in this would come as a fourteen-year-old. I was with my dance teacher, Duggan Hill. At this time, it was so important to be part of a team, performing with local artists for various social causes in Boston. One of the rules for troupe members was that all participants had to show up on time and attend all rehearsals. Another element of our training was the need to always work as a team. All dance groups had to attend their scheduled rehearsals on time and consistently. Failure to meet any of the prerequisites would forfeit our chances to participate in the larger events.

I was so excited at that time. After a year, I had proven that I was serious about my craft. I was on the team, and I had a dance partner, so I felt *official*. During one of our scheduled rehearsals, I was the only one to show up. I was excited to stand in front of the gigantic mirrors to practice dance moves to hip-hop of the early nineties. But my dance partner had decided not to come. After one hour, I sadly grabbed my items and began to make the trek back home. Duggan stopped me and said, "Hey, just because your partner is not here doesn't mean you can't rehearse. You can put the music on and work on your dance numbers."

I replied, "*But my partner is not here.*"

Although it felt awkward, I continued to rehearse. I felt so naked. Soon other people were stopping by and

I was there alone, practicing. This was no fun. I later realized how monumental this lesson was. I learned to value the word *commitment*. I gained the insight that true commitment and passion is enhanced whether or not supporters are there for us. In essence, a lot of my entrepreneurial prowess came from this experience. Subsequently, I would form one of the largest college performing arts group at U of Mass. As the leader of this group, I led events that attracted over two hundred supporters. Truly, practicing the wisdom of isolation had served its purpose as a foundational skill.

We always have times where life tests our dedication. Sometimes we will hear no supportive words to give us the validation we desire. But we still must keep our conviction of living a life of purpose as we move forward.

Questions for Growth:

A. How do you feel when you have to complete a task or project alone?
B. Are you comfortable working in solace?
C. Explain your thoughts here.
D. What is one thing you can do for yourself that is uniquely your sole project?

Time for Restoration

Did you ever wonder why the American bald eagle was selected as the symbol of our country? It was because of its tenacious nature. I can picture the eagle soaring at high altitudes in a clear path to its destination. Years ago, I wrote a poem about the eagle's altitude. It reminded me of how I firmly intended to soar at a higher altitude in my personal life.

Too often, we think about distractions that alter our promise. Too often, we see patterns of doubt or weakness that undermine our goals. Consider this: the same force of nature that carries the eagle can also carry us through transient times in our lives. One stanza from my poem "Fly Like an Eagle" says it all:

Fly Like an Eagle (excerpt)
by Allana Todman-Da Graca

Why don't you fly high?
You're never too old to reach a new destination
Time and longevity have made you scared
Remember, I hold your hand in all seasons
You have to be convinced
Not of what others say
You need to be convinced that I can renew you

The eagle's beak is constantly renewed by the substance keratin. In the same way, our decisions can be consistently patterned, revealing a replenished version of who we desire to become. We may have experienced trauma, setbacks, or deep personal injury, but we can decide to form a new blueprint for our lives. Consider writing an affirmation of how you can focus on the "eagle" journey. While doing this, become detached from those who cannot understand your new journey in life. A season of awakening may beckon you to focus your time on finding new aspects of life.

Questions for Growth:

A. Are you flying at a high altitude in life? What does this look like for you?
B. In what ways would you like to emulate the eagle?
C. Who are the positive individuals who have helped you soar in different areas of your life?
D. When can you find a moment to reflect on the course of your life?

Face Your Authentic Self

What would it mean to actually face your inner truth? This is a tough question to answer. While leading women's groups, I have found many who suffer in isolation with depression. They experience nights of restlessness, wondering whether they are alone in their life challenge. In this emotional space, we feel that nobody understands the hole in our heart that came from abuse, broken relationships, or a lost career opportunity. Sometimes we cannot change because we don't want to hurt someone we love, and we have sacrificed our personhood to avoid confrontation. While this is a useful coping mechanism, it is temporary, something like poking a pin into our own heart. This causes the greatest possible pain because the repressed feelings need to be expressed.

Many women are caretakers and nurturers. These are heroic traits, but they can also be damaging. Many women find it difficult to set strong boundaries or to even mention their limits. I had to realize this for myself. I would find myself, cooking, cleaning, grading, making appointments, and feeling terribly exhausted on a daily basis. At the same time, nobody was forcing me to do this. What was I failing to do? Was I asking for help? Wasn't there a better way for me to meet daily demands without suffocating myself?

Some people repress their desires so much that they develop a list of loved one's wrongdoings. We think that by holding on to this anger, somehow we are hurting the other person. But this is wrong. In essence, we are hurting ourselves. Instead we should consider effective ways to face the truth. Based upon our formative experiences, we are probably unable to make an objective assessment.

For example, if one was picked on as a child, that person may not like confrontation at all. But if one was nurtured in a balanced manner, that person could look at the same situation as an opportunity for improvement. Change is never comfortable. In our efforts to change, we have to look at what still pains us.

It helps to jot down the names of those who have offended us and list the issues we have with them. We can also consider how many hours we have already spent meditating on the wrong that was done. In doing so, we may recognize that we need to face our anger and repressed emotions. After all, if we fail to find closure from our negative experiences, we might make a vow to never allow anyone to hurt us in those ways again. With this in mind, we do not want to forfeit our innate power to deal with difficult situations that warrant action on our part.

Questions for Growth:

A. Are you able to set realistic expectations with family and friends?
B. What are some of the emotions you feel when you fail to say no?
C. Consider to write a reflection about maintaining personal boundaries.

The Gem of Gifts

Motivational speaker Les Brown has always inspired me. He stated that many people die before seeing their dreams come to fruition. I do not believe that anyone starts out by saying, "I am determined *not* to reach my fullest potential."

Unfortunately, our decisions reflect a mosaic of factors that influence the choices we make. This can consist of family influence, job loss, and fear of failure or success. In any event, many individuals in our country are looking for ways to overcome deep dissatisfaction that stems from not reaching personal or professional goals. As an eighth grade teacher, I used to tell my students the following equation:

Conviction + Passion = Purpose

I wanted them to realize that the sooner they found ways to express their inner truths, the sooner they could become stronger adults. I would often use the inspirational story of Matthew Stefanic, a nine-year-old boy who was melting the hearts of America with his poems of encouragement and inspiration. Diagnosed with a life-threatening illness, he was determined to make each day count. While having extensive medical treatment, he still found ways to stay committed to his work. In essence, he warmed and encouraged millions.

All of us have areas of weakness, distraction, or frustration. It's a natural blessing to use our inner gifts to bring peace, encouragement, and care to others. Some people are great at cooking, cleaning, decorating, painting, singing, organizing, acting, speaking, directing, and beyond. Such natural abilities require little effort, for they seem to come naturally. The hardest aspect is having long periods of time without an outlet to express these gifts. I have seen people blame and resent others who decide to pursue something of interest to them. This decision to criticize someone who has decided to move forward actually stems from deep dissatisfaction in the person doing the criticizing. The critical person may have failed to strive for their personal goals due to extensive hours at work, demands of the family, or inactivity in the area of interest. Resentment arises when they realize they have missed out by not pursuing something near and dear.

Granted, there may be times when a rest is needed to recharge our desires, but there needs to be a personal gauge telling us when we are not in line with our personal compass. When we make a commitment to serve in a new area, we will find a renewed sense of purpose and drive that extends beyond ourselves. This, in itself, is like refueling a car that's been running on empty.

Questions for Growth:

A. What are some of your natural gifts?
B. Are you able to use these gifts effectively?
C. What is one way that you may be able to utilize these gifts to serve others?

Day Seventeen: Tomorrow Can't Wait

Facing Our Fears

Sometimes we allow our fears to keep us from achieving our personal potential. Naturally, an element of chance enters any new path, and a situation may not turn out the way we wanted. Additionally, past experience may tell us to avoid taking a step of faith. Again, we feel fear when it comes to beginning a new relationship, business venture, or academic journey. We ask, "How will I know things will work out this time? How long will it take? What happens if this does not work? What will happen if this person agrees or disagrees with my choices?" Questions like these may flood our thoughts. Paradoxically, we may even have a fear of success.

Even if you have moved past these challenges, it may still take time to adjust to different levels of reward for success. I remember an episode of *The Biggest Loser* where a contestant feared singing in public. She was scared to appear in front of the audience because she feared they would perceive her as out of shape and unfit to share her gift of song. *The Biggest Loser* team put her fears to the test and required her to sing the National Anthem to a group of strangers. Initially, she was hesitant to complete this task, but a sense of reward and relief overcame her emotions as she proceeded to sing the song. She was surprised at her own success. Her voice was radiant, and the audience enjoyed her performance.

With this example, think of individuals who naturally exhibit warmth and peace when decorating. They do this with ease where others would require years of training. There are natural chefs, too, who create delicious meals without using a measuring cup to balance the ingredients. In the same predicament, some of us would have burned through two entire meals!

The gifts we naturally possess are gems to be treasured. Every individual has a unique set of fingerprints and a unique personality that is characterized by both strengths and weaknesses. We can choose to utilize these natural gifts in a way that benefits others.

Questions for Growth:

A. What are some of your natural gifts?

B. Are you able to use these gifts effectively?

C. What is one way that you may be able to utilize these gifts to serve others?

Moving from Fear to Transition

Fear is real. Thousands of individuals experience fear of going outside, speaking in a group, or taking a new direction in life. The unknown can wreak havoc on a person's mind. The problem is even more pronounced if someone has experienced major losses. Fear experts contended that the best way to overcome fear is to face it one step at a time. What do you fear? When did you first think of it? Did the fear start with you having a bad experience in the past?

I remember a middle-aged woman who came to one of my women's meetings. She seemed fully engaged, so I was surprised to find that this was the first time that she had been out of her house in six months. She was so afraid of being outside in public that she had even hired a personal assistant to attend the Women Building Confidence Seminar I was teaching. She mustered up enough courage to leave her house, which was forty minutes away, to attend this meeting. She had surprised herself.

Another student had an awesome experience breaking through her fear. This ninth grader was auditioning for a role in a school play. She had been turned down for prior roles because she was too soft-spoken. So I recommended a dramatic role she could practice to develop confidence and speak more clearly. One day she came in for a tutorial.

I looked at her and said, "I want you to think like this particular character. I would like you to scream very loud." She said she couldn't do this, so I urged her to try something different. Abruptly, she let out a loud yell that filled the room. After a moment's silence, her face reflected a level of release. This transformation happened right in front of my eyes!

Something shifted in this student, and she ended up getting one of the lead roles in the play. Her confidence increased and her demeanor became more defined. This is a good example for the rest of us. If we want something different, we may need to try something new. At first, the change may feel overwhelming, but we have to start somewhere. Take small steps to change a perception or behavior. Reward yourself for a job well done.

> If this young lady hadn't taken the small step of attending the meeting, she may have never learned to appear confident in public.

Taking risks for change is very difficult. It may feel safer not to do anything when you are afraid to do something new. The only way to overcome this is by completing tasks that will move you towards reaching your personal and professional goals.

Questions for Growth:

A. What is one trait you do not currently possess that you would like to have?

B. Who is someone who you know who demonstrates this trait?

C. Consider conducting an interview with this role model and getting some tips for gaining confidence in this area.

Dark Alleys, Solo Journeys

I help people move in new directions. But too often they tell me why they just can't do it. I've seen this across the board. Whether it's a female asking about weight loss or a fellow doctoral student asking how he can hurry though the program, they ask, "How did you do it?" But as soon as I begin to talk about overcoming hurdles and trying new strategies, they cut me off and say they have already tried this. Inwardly, I ask myself, *Why are they asking for advice if they do not truly want it?*

Some areas require more work than others. For example, I have referred to my weight loss challenge and the hurdles I had to overcome just to achieve a balanced weight. But that's not enough. Even after losing the weight, I still struggle to maintain a healthy lifestyle.

I remember getting to a healthy weight and telling myself that one cookie here and there was fine. I would eat a small apple pie, saying I'd only have one pie a week. With time, I noticed that I had regained six pounds. I was angry when I saw some of my peers who hadn't gained a pound of fat since high school graduation. It made me angry to know that I had to continue making dietary sacrifices. I was upset so I ate a large bag of potato chips, closing my eyes to the fact that I needed to eat a high-fiber diet.

To escape my self-pity, I thought of the way I came into the world. I was born as a premature baby—just one pound! The doctors had to keep me in the hospital to be treated for nutritional deficiencies, etc. Actually, the odds were stacked against me when it came to survival. Despite this, I developed without any physical ailments.

Indeed, I am reminded that in life we are selected to go through processes we probably would not choose on our own. There are aspects of our journey that are uniquely our own. In the solace of that journey comes an element of surprise and strength that cannot be experienced without hurdles.

When I am able to sing and create, I discover an element of pure connection to something greater than myself that allows me to feel so light and happy that I just can't live without it. This helps me appreciate the dark passageways that I had to traverse in order to achieve my goals.

Questions for Growth:

A. What is one area in your life where you have been successful?

B. What were some of the hurdles that you had to climb over to reach your goal?

C. How can you use this prior experience to encourage you to move forward in other areas of your life?

Day Twenty: Tomorrow Can't Wait

Facing Our Inner Truths

Excuses, excuses! I often sit with students who just can't seem to complete an assignment or project. They describe their struggles, explaining that they aren't physically well. Or they might identify overwhelming personal challenges they haven't had time to deal with. They may have busy schedules, or they may be raising families or tending to additional responsibilities not mentioned here. In our society, we hear such "personal vomit" on a daily basis. I use this term when I refer to the culmination of life challenges that need to be addressed.

Whether we hear of bullying, violence, or protest at an organization, we usually find that the perpetrator has faced serious social and psychological challenges in the past and harbored them for some time. I believe it's healthier to face our inner truths.

Consider asking yourself the tough questions: "What am I resentful of? If I could change one aspect of my life, what would it be? What are some things I desire?" We need to ask these personal questions or we may hide our inner desires behind a mask of external acceptance. Symptoms of this might be nights of restlessness, anxiety about the future, resentment about the past, and inner pains unaccounted for. Unfortunately, many people can't see how important it is to address external challenges that thwart personal and professional goals. Too often, we dismiss obvious truths because they seem less significant than the need for employment, a relationship, or other important factors.

The ability to realistically face our own unique passions may halt the resentment that builds when we have false expectations of others. I am reminded of a popular sitcom from the eighties, *227*, where a couple had begun dating. They were both getting to know each other and did not want to show any weaknesses. By the third date, the initial sparks began to fade and they were involved more deeply. By the end of the date, the gentleman removed his toupee and the woman removed her hair extensions and fake press-on nails. They both stood there in their natural state and decided to accept each other as they really were.

How many of us would dare to stand naked in front of the mirror while pouring out our deepest pains? Many social movements have dared people to face their fears by looking into their hearts. This is where we find the secrets of pain and harbored failure. We can be grateful for the positive aspects of influences that came from our loved ones even as we learn from the negative experiences that have shaped the passions we have today.

Questions for Growth:

A. What is one area of your life that you are not pleased with?
B. List two feelings of resentment that you have.
C. What would it take to remove this frustration?
D. What actions can you take to end the dissatisfaction you presently have?

Encouragement and Positive Influence

It's hard to look at people we love when they have lost that twinkle in their eyes. Thinking of people's behaviors, we come back to the influences that shape our self-perception.

Once, at the beginning of a new semester, I stood before my class and discussed their future assignments. After this, I asked the students to stand up and introduce themselves. One young lady had decided to sit at the back of the classroom, and she refused to look up. During a breakout activity, I asked the students to interview each other, and one classmate approached the student in back, asking why she appeared so withdrawn. The young lady remained quiet and did not say anything. She stayed silent for the first two weeks of class.

One of their assignments was to give an informative presentation about a subject in which they had expertise. For example, if they knew of relatives with a specific disease, career focus, or vocation, they were able to explain this to the class. On the day of the speech the withdrawn student decided to speak on how she had been diagnosed with scoliosis, a situation where the spine has abnormal curvature. She told the class that she never felt beautiful or accepted as a result of her prognosis. In essence, she felt invisible. This person explained why she felt unworthy of beauty and mentioned never wearing dresses or sleeveless outfits because she feared that someone would make fun of her.

As the instructor, I decided to use this speech as an opportunity to challenge her self-perception. I saw her ability to express her perceived weakness to the class as a learning moment. She initially felt withdrawn and isolated because of her self-perception. I asked the class what their thoughts were about her prognosis. I asked if she could change her self-perception. The class appeared as though they wanted to acknowledge her condition. Immediately, hands shot up all over the classroom. Many students offered advice, tips, and personal stories to encourage her.

The next week, she arrived in class with a new hairstyle and beautiful spring dress. The entire class complimented her, and her smile was priceless. Students acknowledged and validated something that was already true about her. She was beautiful on the inside, and now we could see it on the outside. As the term continued, her grades improved, and it made me think how far she could have gone in life if she had enjoyed consistent levels of support and encouragement with regards to her diagnosis.

Questions for Growth:

A. What is one area in your life where your performance has been unsatisfactory?
B. What are some synonyms to describe the emotions you feel?
C. How can you use your support network to help you improve in your weaker areas?

Fear of Success

Thinking over these days while reading this book, are you surprised that our discussion keeps coming back to situations of fear? This is because fear that things may not work smoothly can prevent people from working effectively. Most people do fear failure, but there's another challenge that's surprising: a fear of success. This occurs when someone is unable to accept applause or recognition. For example, the nerd in the classroom may be marginalized for having a brilliant mind. Additionally, a young person who has the desire to be a leader has to endure the gossip or slander of peers. In cases like this, a person can become so accustomed to slander that success is hard to take.

I can recall working with a student whose father was a well-known political figure. When he was with his friends, he would have to be reprimanded or warned for poor behavior and conduct. His academic work was a complete contradiction, for he was very talented and analytical. I asked him about this. He reacted by saying he didn't know why he acted that way. Given his background, I gathered that he didn't want to stand out in a manner that would give him unwanted attention.

Sometimes we can't understand why someone is selected for promotion or an award, but one of their peers is not. Perhaps they are avoiding recognition just because they fear their friends will become jealous and reject them.

Unfortunately, there are other individuals (in the city we call these people "haters") who consistently feel threatened by someone else's impending success. This may be characterized by consistent criticism, downplaying of achievements, or neglecting to give praise or validation to someone who is reaching a particular goal.

We may also sense a lack of support from people we expect to be there for us. This can make us feel it's pointless to strive toward goals. It's like the child who decides to bowl and looks back over his shoulder to see whether he is able to strike all of the pins. He is looking for praise and admiration from the parents or teachers. In such cases, I have noticed that when there is no one to look to for this admiration, the child has a sour look of disappointment. In essence, the desire to feel love and support from close ones can add to the level of confidence that's internalized within an individual.

We do care about how others view us. At the same time, it's important to have discretion when it comes to sharing successful opportunities. Regardless of recognition, we desperately desire the feeling of contentment that comes from working hard toward a particular goal.

Questions for Growth:

A. Consider reflecting on your prior responses to "Questions for Growth" in this book. Circle the themes that repeat in your journal entries.

B. What can you learn from the persistent traits that characterize themselves in your moment of reflection?

Day Twenty-Three: Tomorrow Can't Wait

The Gift of Letting Go!

The journey of life brings many uphill battles.

Let's face it, one can simply turn on the television set and witness the routine portrayal of heinous crimes. Prime time news often includes violence between loved ones. Such reports make me wonder how loved ones of the victims cope. Additionally, there are life events where there is no particular person to blame, and this can be strikingly traumatic. When the earthquake hit in Haiti, I was baffled because some people had lost entire families. In the same way, traumatic events involving verbal, physical, and sexual abuse can severely damage the self-view and development of an individual.

I asked some of my students to describe how they had been influenced as children. One young lady reported that she had been adopted in her late teens. This was fine, but she felt shocked and confused when her parents gave special treatment to her brother, their biological son. She took this as a direct slap to her self-worth. It left her with feelings of brokenness. Lacking encouragement, she lost her ability to believe she could ever complete anything successfully. This left feelings of resentment and hostile anger, which came to overshadow all of her positive attributes.

Often, individuals who have endured abuse as young people are unable to halt recurring memories of these hurtful events, which can be characterized as Post Traumatic Stress Disorder. Harboring repressed feelings may trigger PTSD and cause a rollercoaster of emotions. This may cause awkwardness, making them feel inadequate, threatening their confidence.

In my case, I recalled being mistreated and feeling absolutely hopeless. One example of this was when I was a musician as a high school student. I was excited because I was able to record my first song ever. Excited about this, I decided to play this song for all to hear at a social gathering. A random adult and his girlfriend were listening to the soundtrack and decided to make a comment. "It doesn't matter how good this sounds," they said. "She's black and ugly."

First, I was shocked because this man was not exactly eye candy either. Second, he was an *adult* and, under most conventions, young people are taught to respect and value the opinions of adults. Consistent experiences like this led me to question my abilities. Truly, I doubted my ability to sing based on this person's interpretation of my beauty. It was as if I had internalized my treatment to mean that I could not succeed.

Habitual experiences like this made me *feel* like a victim. I can even recall when I was barely able to get up and put my clothes on. It was hard to feel good about myself when I felt so yucky inside.

I am also reminded of *New York Times* bestselling author Dave Pelzier, who has spoken publicly about the abuse he endured at the hands of his mother. As outsiders, we want to know what made his mother turn her precious son into an object. He recounts the negative words and physical actions that his mother had toward him. Despite his difficult upbringing, he remained open to receiving love. The relationship with his mother was never glossy in the end, but he was able to let the deep disappointment of a shaky relationship with her go. When she was close to her death, he was able to have a discussion with her without harboring feelings of resentment and regret. He felt a steady peace that kept him emotionally stable.

This is especially promising because it leads me to see that we can proactively face our past with gratitude, overcoming the weight of our painful experiences. We may no longer invite the person who hurt us to our dinner table, but we also no longer want to drag them in the mud when we see them. We can take our power back by looking at what matters the most to us.

We can become grateful just for waking up with a roof over our heads. We may choose to be grateful for those who contribute to us by building our spirits up and helping us strive ahead. Fortunately, we can follow the advice of the aforementioned authors, for they conducted research and found that individuals who devoted time to deal with their losses through prayer were consequently able to decrease their PTSD and levels of resentment. We can begin to look at our pain and acknowledge that the individuals who caused us harm really have no influence on what we can become in life. Indeed, there is much work to do.

Questions for Growth:

A. What are your thoughts on forgiveness?
B. What are two experiences that have challenged you to pardon someone from hurting you in the past?
C. Consider journaling a letter of forgiveness to the person who caused you pain.

Day Twenty-Four: Tomorrow Can't Wait

Let the Apple Be the Apple!

When I counsel women, caring for them and desiring to point them in the right direction, it's difficult to help them prevent the poor choices they seem bound to make. On a smaller level, we can see why a teacher would stop toddlers from repeatedly pulling candy from the jar for fear of sugar toxicity. Later, as a person begins to mature and age, such guidance from mentors or outsiders can be unwelcomed because people just want to make their own choices.

I have learned through many exchanges with women that the best thing to do is to listen. Often, experience is the best teacher. But sometimes learning from negative experiences can be unbearable.

The hardest of these experiential truths seem to stem from relationships. I have discovered this through personal experience and working with women: when you have a dream and a prayer for someone who has not constructed a concretized view of themselves, there is potential for *huge* disappointment!

In my Speech Communication classes, we discuss the values we place on aspects of our lives, be they family, spirituality, church, career, friendships, or legacy. Many students are unaware why we are doing this until I explain that their values may be driving their perceptions and subsequent decisions.

In one class I may say, "All of you in here have various values that are unique to your character. There is no right or wrong list of values, for each of you have different attitudes. This is important to consider because, as we communicate with others, we need to exchange feelings about these values. This way we can have integrity in the midst of conversation and maintain a balance of perspective. Acknowledging that the priorities of others are not in exact alignment with our own can help us gauge the type of individuals with whom we can develop intimate relationships."

I further tell students, "For example, why would I bite an apple and hope it tastes like an orange? Either we respect the person or object as it is or we will be consistently frustrated."

This can cause great debate and lively discussion. Students often come to the consensus that this understanding is harder to put into practice than they expected. I remember an adult learner who gave a speech about domestic violence in class. She described the abuse she had suffered at the hands of her child's father. At the end of her presentation, she said she was working on leaving this individual as she realized he was physically abusive and not able to treat her in a respectful manner. As the semester went on, this student stopped coming to class. She called me once in the middle of the night, and I reminded her how valuable she was. I reminded her that, once she saw her own beauty and value, she could take mini steps to accept the idea of having a relationship with someone who valued her. After this call, another six months went by.

I eventually saw this student on crutches with dark shades on as she tried to get life started all over again. I asked her how she was doing, but, sadly, the conversation confirmed that she was still with the person and not sure how to transition out. She probably had hopes that this individual would eventually treat her with the respect she deserved. Unfortunately, her sanity and physical health were compromised by her choice to return to an unproductive relationship.

I have met many women like this. They have sacrificed being loved due to the fear of being alone. I have also heard stories of a man cheating on his spouse, but wanting to maintain status quo by appearing like the perfect gentleman to others. These women have shared their secrets with me, and I have kept their stories in my heart, but inwardly I want them to have enough faith to know that they are worth more than they think. This is the hardest to bear.

Believe me, I have also had my fair share of heartache. In my young adult years, I learned these lessons as well. I learned, in relationships in general, that people will often show us their values by what they choose to do. I have learned to value the time it takes to observe the actions of an individual. After expressing my concerns, I leave it up to the individual to respond with actions that show their level of care for me.

My process was not as easy as it may seem. As a college student, my true friends warned me about making poor choices. In my angst, I ignored them and then eventually regretted not heeding their advice. Indeed, when we bite an apple, we expect it to taste like one. To have any other expectation is to lie to ourselves.

Questions for Growth:

A. What have you learned about relationships from reading this excerpt?
B. Do you have realistic expectations of your friends?
C. What was a negative experience you had with one of your friends?
D. What did you learn from this experience?
E. Is your relationship with this person reciprocated?

Defying the Odds

Now that I'm approaching my midthirties, I notice advertisements telling me how to soothe the aches and pains of growing older. For me, the message is, "Allana, you are getting *older.*"

Society seems to expect us to just settle down with age and abandon our favorite dreams. What a contrast to the energy, passion, and enthusiasm of our high school and college days, when we were encouraged to grasp the future and reach for our dreams. Now, even in my thirties, I find that this cheerleading squad of mentors is fading into the background.

For example, I remember how shocked we were when Susan Boyle stood soberly in front of an audience and sang "I Dreamed a Dream" from the soundtrack of *Les Miserables.* She was past her thirties, not wearing the latest trends, but when she opened her mouth, a passion emerged from inside and captured our hearts. Many were moved to tears.

We may face many challenges when we try to maintain youth and vigor. Indeed, as I grow older, I recognize a need to make a daily choice so I will keep my childhood passions strong. On the negative side, if we have gained weight or lost time due to work or family schedules, we may feel that it's too late for us.

Think of it this way. The average American watches at least twenty-five hours of television a week. If we add the time we spend on the telephone, social media, or excessive extracurricular activities, we can see that we have more time than we think. We find time to spend money on items we like and travel to special destinations, and even this confirms that we can strive to do things if we set our mind to it.

One of my workout buddies has been a real inspiration. When she started working out, she weighed in close to three hundred pounds. She was a few months away from getting a gastric bypass to drop her weight. But first she decided to sign up with a personal trainer and to workout consistently. It was really tough for her, for she needed to cook for three kids while she learned about health and nutrition.

That's when I met her in one of my personal training sessions. As time went on, she lost well over one hundred pounds. Today we laugh at the number of admirers who are now praising her for her persistence. We both acknowledge that the hardest work is often behind closed doors.

Working out together was awesome. We kept each other accountable and spurred each other on during sessions. Interestingly, there were many people who started with us but they eventually stopped coming. Why did they stop? Again, they mentioned their work schedules or inability to get to the gym on time. Half of the battle is overcoming your internal conversations.

When I felt stagnant in my workout routine, I would buy a new sport suit as an incentive. I would also watch a good health video about nutrition before eating lunch. Whenever I chose to eat what the physician recommended, it would pump me up and leave me feeling like I had accomplished something special.

Recently, we returned from a trip to Africa. We were visiting friends of family in Gabon, where the mother was set apart from the party because she had Alzheimer's disease. As the crowd dimmed dwindled, the music continued to play, and Grandma wanted to join in on the action. It was so beautiful to see this woman, ninety-eight years old, dance to her favorite songs as women held her up for support. Every time these women thought she was finished, a new song would start and this woman would beckon with her hips that she wanted to dance more. She must have danced for seven songs. The women holding her were excited and tired from holding on, but the spirit of this lady surpassed her age. She was youthful in her movements and determined to have her fun!

Nobody knows us like we know ourselves. We have the power to meet our mental challenges and proactively put a plan in place to overcome the hurdles of transformation. Age is just a number. How we treat ourselves governs how well we exemplify our age.

Unforgiveness: Are There Uninvited Guests at the Kitchen Table?

My doctoral research on learner's persistence had interesting results. In that study, I discovered many circumstances where students had just behaved in the way their mentors expected. This is great when the person takes a positive view and the students acquiesce to the goal of performing well. Unfortunately, some studies have reported that educators *sometimes have negative preconceptions* about a student's success and these can become actualized by the end of the term. This produces an expectation that the student will not perform well.

Nonverbal communication can strongly influence an individual's success or failure. Now, don't get me wrong: by no means do I blame educators for this. What's important is that internalization of these thoughts can become troublesome.

Motivation research shows that outside influences have an effect on individual motivation. For example, some individuals thrive on attention received from others. They may like to volunteer, participate in speaking activities, or lead a team of people because they feel alive helping others. Additionally, some are driven by intrinsic means, and their motivation to complete a task is based on a connection from a deeper place.

For example, a woman may volunteer at an orphanage because she can relate to being a foster child. Another person may find that spiritual beliefs drive the choices he makes. In essence, a balance is needed.

I have this problem myself. Despite all of the workshops, seminars, courses, and articles I write, I often have to make sure I am not just bringing people that hurt me to my kitchen table. In my work, there will always be someone who may question a statement or suggestion that I have made. There may be times when I share an idea and it may not be received well. This may lead to a workshop where people may be less inclined to engage in discussion. Now, I could walk away from this scenario feeling discouraged that the time spent in the workshop was useless. This same pattern can happen with interpersonal relationships.

If I have closed the door on an unproductive relationship but still harbor resentment, bitterness, and anger toward this person by replaying the negative moments in my mind, then I know I have invited a negative force into my intimate environment. In this case, the person's effect on me today will be just like it was in the past.

I once heard a voice reminding me that I failed to let certain painful experiences go. I really felt that by repeating, rehearsing, and recalling these horrific moments, I would be protected from further harm. It took a long time to realize that this was wreaking havoc on my mental and spiritual health. My hands were in an invisible fist, which held me back from receiving all that I was inviting others to share: love, hope, opportunity, and a chance for new dreams and life journeys to begin.

I once vowed never to be hurt again. Since then, some of my friends would remind me that I needed to forgive myself for breaking that vow. This made no sense to me. Why would I ask forgiveness for something I didn't do to myself? I realized that it wasn't wise to place demands on things I would not do. I began to harbor unrealistic expectations for others and myself. I even became angry and found it difficult to be compassionate toward those who had hurt me.

I actually decided to piggyback on a lesson explained on Day Twenty-Four: Let the Apple Be the Apple! This was to place the individuals who had caused great pain into the atmosphere. I released the pain from the years when I used to suffer bullying and rejection.

As a result, I now feel lighter and sober in thought. I have even taken a moment to send positive thoughts toward those who have harmed me. Pain is no longer invited to my kitchen table.

Questions for Thought:

A. Close your eyes and picture yourself forgiving the one who hurt you the most.
B. Consider feeling the corresponding emotions of this hurt.
C. See yourself letting the person and their behavior go.

Making Every
Moment Count

Wow! Today I had a meeting with my girls' group at a local library. Normally, five to six girls come to gain skills in self-esteem and confidence, but today only two girls showed up.[1] I was really unsure what to share with them, but I felt we should continue to address hurt, decision-making, and self-awareness. The session began with the girls highlighting what they had learned during the prior week. I told them my story about pulling up weeds from our life (see Day Eight of this book).

I asked the girls to write the word *forgiveness* on a piece of paper. After some discussion, we all agreed that this term meant the ability to pardon someone who had wronged and hurt us. I wanted to go deeper. I asked the girls to write down a range of emotions that they felt throughout that day. They began to write:

Happy
Sad
Anger

---

[1]   It was awesome to see the light bulb turn on for these girls. They saw that, if they continue to internalize these thoughts and allow the negative views of people to get to them, it could thwart their opportunities to become their best selves. Amazingly, there were only two participants, and yet this was a great "a-ha" moment for me.

Fear
Anxiety
Mad

Then I asked them to rate their levels of emotion from 1–10. (One meant never feeling this emotion and ten meant always feeling it.) Each girl mentioned the emotions and highlighted her reason for feeling this way. Naturally, we came to the subjects of gossip, backbiting, shaming, and more. Now, between the three of us, we were really getting somewhere. So I proceeded to have the girls draw a circle that represented their brains.

Against this background, the girls could show how they had suffered hurt from someone and, worse yet, had come to *internalize* that person's attitudes as true. I wanted to show them that, despite their impending unhappiness, they could still choose how long they would stay in that dissatisfied state of mind. I explained, "You have to remind yourself that every moment you spend thinking, rehearsing, and harnessing pain, you are robbing yourself of opportunities to have positive experiences."

One girl replied, "Dr. D, I am keeping this paper because I have to put this quote on my wall." Indeed, something had touched this girl.

Isn't it funny that the more we dwell on something, the more it may lead us to make poor choices?

For example:

Tina may feel sad, and this may lead her to choose not to go out and socialize. Sadly, this may give her a negative outlook on life.

Ed may feel poor and begin to steal because he fears not having anything. Then, inadvertently, he might become characterized as a thief.

Questions for Growth:

A. Who do you still bring to your *kitchen table*?
B. What are some ways that has impacted your level of joy?
C. How can you release the inner pain that this has caused you?
D. Consider making a list of the people you hold resentment toward.
E. Complete a 1–2 page writing exercise to expose your thoughts about these feelings and individuals. Then, throw this item away once you are ready to release these experiences.

Day Twenty-Eight: Tomorrow Can't Wait

Saying No to Commitments for Health and Wellness

Isn't it interesting when we encounter an alcoholic or drug addict? We can say, "Wow, just look at them. They are so messed up. I'm glad I'm not like them." Ironically, addiction isn't the only problem. For example, some of us are addicted to overworking. This can be just as damaging to the psyche as a more visible control issue.

Actually, when we lack a full picture of what that person is going through, we tend to make incorrect assumptions. For example, I think of people who volunteer to be on every board or council in town. They always seem willing to partake in activities, leaving no time for anything else. They actually seek to be consumed, energized, led, or preoccupied with something.

I had some of these traits myself. In the past, I found myself joining many social causes. Even in college, where achievement was noted as honorable, I tried to do it all. In one semester, I became the diversity director for the college radio station and the *Black Affairs* contributor for the UMass Daily Collegian as well as an advocate for student affairs. I was so busy that I literally had no time to organize pamphlets, flyers, journal entries, and writings that stemmed from my work. I just had failed to master the ability to say no!

Why did I do this? I was masking an internal void by signing up for everything. As long as I was busy, I did not need to think about my personal life. I felt safest being busy. However, my addiction to the adrenaline rush made it impossible to live at ease. Yes, I received praise and accolades for my work. In all of it, however, I remember feeling that I could never be quite satisfied after completing a task. Somehow, right after a major accomplishment, I was ready to tackle the next huge goal. I had almost as much drive as my pet cats have after they eat a Temptations snack. I always wanted more.

Sadly, this continual desire for more can be destructive if not harnessed appropriately. I remember waking up at one point, writing in a journal, going to a social meeting, grading papers, and all the while breathing like I had just ran a marathon. I recall working in the day as a community organizer and serving young girls in the evening, forgetting to eat dinner beforehand and gobbling a meal at a fast food restaurant. I was giving so much of myself to others, but I was not taking care of myself.

Now I have changed. I have come to accept the value of being content in stillness. Unfortunately, meditation does not come naturally for me. For example, today I walked around the park and observed the stillness of nature. Amazingly, I have seldom appreciated how serene and beautiful it is to not have any expectations or goals to meet. It was great to be still and to take in the awesome sounds of chirping birds and the wind blowing in the trees. Every now and then, I would have to remind myself not to *think.*

We need to stop whenever we can and reevaluate our motives and the reasons behind our choices. I realize that the story of the tortoise and the hare has something to teach us. I am learning that, although I am interested in a thousand things, I have the ability to prioritize which tasks or projects can be completed while maintaining levels of peace.

I now accept this type of maturity as a safeguard against frivolous business that is accompanied by the fear of not doing enough. Instead, my hope is to accept each new day with enough energy to accomplish just one meaningful task on the way to an overarching goal. In the long run, when I arrive at the goal, I have the peace of knowing I completed a project that did not sap all of my energy.

Questions for Growth:

A. How is your time management?

B. Are you able to say no to an overwhelming task?

C. When is the last time you had a day to do absolutely *nothing*?

D. Consider taking time to plan a fun day for yourself.

Day Twenty-Nine: Tomorrow Can't Wait

Seeping Bottles

So much can happen in twenty-nine days. My plan was to write this book in thirty days, but it really took time to absorb and process so much information. I have even highlighted my times with Hubster, but this entry was just as significant as other notes describing my time together with you, my reader.

This year, one of our family goals was to get better acquainted with our city. We love to travel, but usually end up just hanging around the house and watching a movie. So, this year we determined that we would attend the symphony.

We went to see *A King Remembrance* with Musical Director Robert Spano. Collaborations that the Atlanta Symphony Orchestra decided to showcase for the evening made this night electric for me. The opening featured an awesome premier of a high school student's creation, a song entitled "Triumph by Day" by Commodore Primous III. It also included the world premiere of a musical piece, "Spirit of the Blues," written by Marcus Roberts. Both of these local artists were given opportunities to create works of inspiration. These were transformed by the symphony into melodic sounds sending waves of emotion that screamed of love, passion, and pain.

Surprisingly, in the crux of these sounds, I saw the image of a water bottle. Water was slowly seeping out. In the background, a voice was saying, "Be careful to watch the seeping bottle. Our lives are full of challenges. These experiences must be addressed. They can slowly rob us from living the rich lives we want."

What an analogy! Life is like purchasing a bottle of water. We would not expect to find a small hole in the bottle. And, just when we need it most, we take a sip, but ... there is no water left. The symphony played a melody of trumpets, drums, violins, and more. It all reminded me that the journey to let go and forgive is just like that seeping bottle. We may think we are holding institutions, individuals, or loved ones responsible by not letting our pain go, but actually, we are draining from the very source we need the most: our inner awareness.

Surprisingly, in that concert, although Marcus Roberts was blind, his fingers floated on the piano in a timeless and effortless way. In his life, he must have struggled to find a way to look beyond his disability so he could see in another way: physically, by feeling vibrations from sounds on his fingertips.

Keep your bottle of life full so that when you need to stop and be refreshed, there's enough left to move you along to your next moment.

Questions for Growth:

A. Do you see your life as half empty or half full?
B. What would be the distractions in your life that are seeping water from your bottle?
C. Consider viewing your life as a bottle without seeping water.

Being Still:
Less Is More

Busy is normal in our fast-paced society. Our increasingly digitized world offers benefits as well as challenges. We can communicate more easily with loved ones and colleagues. But we seem over-indulged in "blings" chiming from our phones. This is just a small example of how we are becoming consumed by technology.

Interestingly, the dictionary highlights a synonym of *consume*: to waste away. Let's not waste the effort of reading these daily entries. How can we change if we can't find a consistent method of being still?

This topic came up when I was speaking to a mentor. She asked me how I spent my time. She wondered whether I relaxed enough. I explained to her that relaxing was difficult for me. I said that, even in moments of resting, I would be consumed with thoughts about what I had to do next or what I could be doing better. In this discussion, I came to the conclusion that I needed to go outside and listen. Then, I would take the advice I heard in a recent church service: to just take a Sabbath.

Usually, I have a goal when I think of going outside. I will run three miles, I will garden, etc. But this time I wanted to make sure I would just *be*. The first ten minutes were great. Then I found my mind wondering. Once this occurred, I said to myself, "Okay, Allana, focus only on the clouds … focus only on the trees. Observe and simply be moved to do nothing."

It felt truly weird. I continued to lie outside on the deck and look up. Then my mind wandered into the clouds, and I became aware of the vastness of the earth where we are blessed to live. I saw birds flying with their families to the next tree. I saw a rabbit playing hide-and-go-seek in the bushes. I felt the sun's rays beaming on my skin. Indeed, it was beautiful just to be.

I also thought how quiet and apparently boring all of this nature seemed to be. In that moment, I was reminded of how we feel when we lay a loved one to rest. After a small few moments, we put them into the ground in a cemetery. At this time, we realize how we are aligned with this earth and the plants that shoot up from the ground.

The body is buried in the ground where insects have lives that are interjected into every pocket of soil below. They live and breathe and feed their colonies of ants. How fascinating it all is. So, why do people wait until they pass away to rest peacefully? I know this is a tough question, but it did convince me.

From that moment, I resolved that times of stillness could be very productive. I planned to remember how I used to feel great after listing the thirteen-odd tasks I had completed in one day. Don't get me wrong: being productive is good. But resting the brain also has psychological and emotional benefits.

Sunday was the day I planned to rest. I normally would not start grading papers until evening, but I realized I was working just as much on this day. Again, being a married woman and a professional had challenges. Should I try to be the *Leave It to Beaver* wife from the old days, striving to be the next Hillary Clinton or the others?

Balance is the key here. I would find myself striving to cook six times over the weekend. Truly, it was only housework, but I would be just as tired as if I had done a full day of work. No one was forcing me to do this. My husband told me to take a break, but for some reason I would compete with myself. Well, I am happy to say that these last two weeks have been very restful.

This past Sunday, I did not cook at all. I cooked the Sunday meal on Saturday night and combined this with extra side items I had prepared the prior week. I promised myself I would work hard to have fun. It was awesome. I took a two-hour nap. I took a long bubble bath. I ate my prized chocolate chip cookies and took another nap before dinner. I was not even aware that my husband had come in and turned the television off.

Wow! I was not sure why I had never done this before. Indeed, the power of rest cannot be understated. I was able to think more clearly and have a mind-set of gratitude while we dined.

Questions for Growth:

A. In your week, count all of the spare time you have in your schedule. Next, write the following question: "How many hours of rest do I get in my spare time?"
B. Are you content with this amount of rest each week?
C. What can you do to add more rest to your week?

Stillness:
I Will Be Happy When

As you might expect, life may not turn out how you planned it. It's a myth from television reality shows and dramas. In reality, the beginning, middle, and end of life are not set in stone. Our life path is sequenced in a unique pattern of time.

For example, when I read the journal entries I wrote back in my early twenties, I find my list of goals in chronological order. At that time, I planned to have:

- a master's degree
- a good job
- a husband
- a house
- kids
- my own business
- miles of world travel
- status as an author
- enough money to pay bills
- accomplishment of my goals by the age of thirty

While I have already accomplished many of these items, I also planted a lot of "should" items, which brought constant pressure. Yes, I was happy to graduate. I was also happy that God blessed me with hubby and we are able to live happily in our present home. Yes, I am excited about eventually becoming a parent, and I'm presently an entrepreneur, but I've always suffered a lack of fulfillment that came from this thought: "I will be happy when …"

We have all said it: "I will be happy when I graduate. I will be happy when I get married. I will be happy when I have that child. I will be happy when I lose that weight." What I have found is that, on a daily basis, I'm always confronted with the choice between effort and contentment.

Usually, in setting goals, we neglect to add that we should anticipate moments of disappointment and hurt. We may fail to see that our job has a glass ceiling and this could challenge us to move into a better position. We may be blessed with a husband but be challenged to work on communicating or bonding as the years progress. We may want to travel the world but have trouble even standing in long lines to go through airport security. We may have enough money to pay the bills, but our love for spending may pose a challenge. Additionally, life still happens as we strive toward these goals. The thought that life will be as smooth as a car commercial is just not reality.

If we have realistic expectations, we can move beyond the "I will be happy when" moments, because we will remember to take one day at a time. Many people say they loved the journey of getting to a new place in life. This was hard for me to accept as a high school student because I was not mature enough to understand. Naturally, I thought instant gratification was most important.

We see the error of thinking this way about gratification when we ponder the natural biology of life. We cannot receive the benefit of a vast garden of life if we have not cleared the negative weeds of experience from our life. People may not notice this until a number of life events occur. For example, an individual with repressed anger about a pertinent relationship, may break out in an outburst of rage. The person they were communicating with may not have seen this anger until the rage ensued. Taken together, we have to be vigilant about the types of people we place in our lives. We cannot conquer our emotions if we refuse to remove thorns of negative people choking our momentum. We cannot successfully gain more if we cannot take care of what we can presently afford.

I am learning that happiness and contentment are a decision. It's an acknowledgment that life will have challenges as well.

Sometimes, in moments of stillness, we may find that deep-seeded emotions rise to the surface. I mentioned the journey I had with an impending illness. This problem led me to routinely visit doctors. With the economy in a state of flux, I was balancing my work with my doctoral research, and at times this was overwhelming. There were moments when I felt stifled in school.

Writing a doctoral thesis takes time. I started to feel annoyed about the impatient rules I had set for myself. The process of writing revisions, waiting for feedback, and deleting elements of writing that did not fit with the research would often distract me from my purpose of completing the doctoral program. In addition, I had to constantly remind myself to be more patient and grateful for opportunities to serve others. My colleagues and I would often gripe about how much longer we had to go in our studies. I began to change my statement in an effort to be objective. I would gently say, "At this point, I am not concerned how long this dissertation will take, but I hope to have gone beyond one more milestone this term." In essence, I learned to appreciate the baby steps made toward reaching each academic goal.

Questions for Growth:

A. Write two or three statements that begin with "I will be happy when …"
B. Why would having these items make you happy?
C. What are ways you can appreciate the moment you are in presently?

Day Thirty-Two: Tomorrow Can't Wait

Mars Moments

Some people say, "Come back to Mars," when someone says something that seems outrageous. As someone blessed with an array of talents (piano, voice, dance, aerobics, public speaking), I find this to be an area in which I need to remain focused. As an artist and educator, I am baffled when trying to choose among various interests. On one hand, I love to teach, instruct, and guide students. On the other hand, I love to engage and use movement and creativity, through plays, songs, and poetry, to enlighten others. But sometimes there just isn't enough time for me to participate in both of these vocations as I would like. I wrote the following in my journal several years ago:

> *This whole term, I have been striving to have my weekends free. Anticipated harder days in the week and worked to focus on difficult days. This week alone, I had numerous tasks at work and classes, completing final presentations and exams. On top of this, I have to deal with student emotions and reactions. I love my job but sometimes it steals from my creative energy. Where has my creative energy gone and what can I do to restore it?*

Although I was able to restore my creative energy by starting this book, I still had a Mars moment creep up this past week. I will give you an example. I dedicated my time to writing this book from a desire deep in my heart. In fact, I am happy that we are at this point because the book is almost over. Well, yesterday I was having a workout session alone and immediately had a flashback of myself touring with a dance troupe with which I used to act. Although I was working out in the living room, I said, "Stage left," "Stage right," and "Down stage" in my head. I saw the chorus line of actors following a choreographed routine of my creation. Immediately, my mind said, "Tomorrow I will be in a dance company." Sweating like I had just left the stage of *Dancing with the Stars*, I went and declared to hubby in his office that I wanted to start a dance company.

He said, flatly, "Honey, finish your book!"

I was upset. I wanted him to react like a fellow performing artist. I wanted to talk about our dreams and the latest artists I had listened to for inspiration. But one of my husband's greatest strengths is business development rhetoric and direction. He reminded me of my goals and intentions for the book. Initially, I was upset with him. I asked myself, "Does he see my heart? Is he like one of those dream snatchers, not caring if I'm sixty-five before I hit the stage again?"

Gradually, I realized that his advice was to remain focused on initial projects. I set out to do this. I needed to calm my anxiety about reaching my goals. He carefully explained how important it was to discern the proper timing and orchestration of goals. I walked away a little disappointed, for I could not put *Flashdance* into action immediately, but I also appreciated his stewardship in helping me remain focused and steady.

You probably can tell that I was never one of those little children that color inside the lines—quite the opposite. However, once a plan of action is decided upon, it is important to remember the trajectory you have initially planned. In order to be productive and effective, it is essential to take time to build upon the nature of a desired skill. Once we have mastered one area, we can venture out to the next.

To avoid Mars moments in daily life, we can rely on those who love us and have our best interests in mind. We can bounce ideas off of them. Ultimately, the decision to be focused or scattered is ours alone.

Questions for Growth:

A. Have you had a time where you had more than one interest at heart?
B. How did you prioritize which activity to pursue?
C. Look at your schedule this week and remove the least important activity from your To Do list.

Day Thirty-Three: Tomorrow Can't Wait

Self-Determination

I am baffled when I think of the children who are abandoned in our nation and world. Not just orphans or foster children. I also think of droves of teenagers. I have heard countless stories of young people who suffer stress, anxiety, disappointment, and lack of love as a result of their family situation. I was particularly moved when one student had nobody from his family at his high school graduation. Yet he was strong. He mentioned to the class that, although no one was present, he himself was present, and he decided that he would receive his degree with pride.

Sometimes we may feel disappointment if we seek love from individuals who just don't love us the way we expect them to. This can become gut-wrenching and hurt us to our core. On the brighter side, some students experience the most unimaginable circumstances and yet develop thick skin that allows them to overcome challenges. I have seen the development of self-determination on a soul level, and this can be accomplished in several ways:

1) Praying for those who have hurt us
2) Releasing them by choosing to complete one or all of the activities in this book
3) Having a level of compassion despite the maltreatment we have suffered

In essence, we can decide to renew ourselves and be healed from past pains by daring to view our best possible selves. Here, in our best selves, we can move past our pain and redeem those who may not even deserve our attention. When we forgive and move forward, we still have a chance to invite someone to have a seat at our table. We also have a choice to take our blinders off and understand how someone's behavior fell into a certain relational pattern.

If behaviors toward us were poor and unjust, we can vow to decide how we would like to be treated. We can create a new mantra exemplifying the beautiful person God created us to be. In that best self, we can find inner peace and become more gracious toward others.

Denial is never a friend. The best way to gain this determination is to take small steps, focusing on how we would like to be treated. We can use the weight of our pain to build up our inner resolve.

Additional Thoughts for Growth:

Create Your Personal Mantra

I (state your name) will be committed to building my esteem, sense of freedom, and self-awareness today.

I (state your name) will be praying for the following people :_____.

I will be respected and treated with dignity.

Affirmation of a Survivor

I am delivered from scattered thinking. My yes will be yes, and my no will be no.
I will not be unsettled by people, situations, family, or friends
I will love myself.
God's best is in me, and I will not be in lack.
I will be treated with dignity and will create boundaries to protect my inner child.
Those who remind me of my past flaws and are not able to treat me with honor have no place in my newness.

(Adapted from *Temple: Self-Discovery of Truth,*
Dr. Allana Da Graca)

Isolation Brings Introspection

Like thousands of Americans who post their early morning surprises or rants, I posted the following on my Facebook page:

Just because I may be down and going through something does not mean I am always going to be there. With isolation there comes introspection and only the wisdom that the one above can give. When there is no counsel, I know who I can call. Amen.

I decided to share this because I recognize that when we "Face" our life in an intense forty-day journey like this, we may feel overwhelmed with the self-awareness we gain from journaling and having deep reflection. Feelings of sadness, anger, excitement, and angst can ensue and make us feel as though no progress is being made. This makes me reflect on a sign I ran across as I was driving.

I was sitting at a stop sign and looked to my right while I waited for the light to change. There was a big sign that said the land was under construction. The sign warned that crews would be demolishing, clearing debris, and paving a new foundation. Ironically, the sign depicted a method to navigate through life's trials.

Similarly, in our lives we may feel that we are in a demolition phase. Our thoughts may feel scattered as we think of those who caused discontentment. But, as we use this book as a launch pad to a brighter future, we may want to refine and organize our thoughts and develop a strategy to move forward in life. With truthfulness and honesty, we can pave a new foundation for a brighter future.

What can be frustrating is the thought that real change can occur, like a get-rich-quick scheme, but this is far from the truth. True change takes time. We all love the way home shows conduct renovations because we know that what is revealed in the end was worth the initial demolition. Do not be discouraged by the sense of discord you may feel from getting at the root of life's challenges. Change is coming.

Questions for Growth:

A. What are the top two learning moments you have experienced since reading this book?
B. How do you feel now that you have addressed these areas in your life?
C. What has this transformation meant for you?
D. Who can you share this newfound learning with?

Day Thirty-Five: Tomorrow Can't Wait

Welcome Change

With all our discussion about facing our past and our problems, I cannot fail to bring up the topic of change. Change can be welcomed and abhorred at the same time. With transition comes an unusual responsibility: accepting the idea that change is a natural process. In life we may make a new start with employment, relationship partners, or organizations where we can volunteer. The initial excitement can increase or slowly lead to stagnation. Both perspectives can come with a mental price.

I have found that personal change moves forward in phases. First, I feel a bit of discomfort from the daily regimen of completing a familiar task. Later, I notice a dull internal voice that tells me how bored and dissatisfied I am. When this occurs, I ask myself, "Am I in a moment of growth or am I in a place where I have already learned all the lessons I am supposed to learn?"

In the next phase, I have a choice to let those I am connected to know that I will no longer be participating in the assigned group, project, or task at hand. Again, in this moment of making my choice, I have an opportunity to feel guilty and shameful for letting down those that I care about. It's very difficult.

I have learned that people-pleasing is not effective for anyone. If one stays in a place of stagnancy for the sake of comfort, resentment seems to be the only gift that is given in return.

Questions for Thought:

A. Are you presently growing in your personal or professional life?
B. Do you think you have learned everything that you should in this place?
C. What would you like to do differently?

Developing the Best Self

When we adopt an attitude of *best self*, we accept that, beyond previous experience, misfortune and inflicted pain are still likely to exist in our future. Despite this reality, we can ignite an improved life through prayer and meditation. In this way, we can accept the grace extended to us in the form of natural gifts, nature, and moments of awareness.

If someone has been abandoned by their parents, they may feel extreme levels of isolation and despair. Even thoughts of suicide can form in these individuals, and it's vital for them to realize that these thoughts really do matter. If someone has lost mobility due to an accident or illness, they may feel levels of resentment and bitterness. I remember my brother asking me, "Would you dance if you lost your legs?"

I said, "I guess I would have to write instead."

Then he asked, "What about if you lost your hands?"

I replied, "I guess I would have to use my voice." Indeed, as hard as any of these circumstances may be, we have an opportunity to rise above the problem.

Thinking of the teachers, role models, and authority figures that influenced me, I am reminded to focus on their best intentions, as well as their faults, with a level of compassion. Like it or not, I have to release any negative memories that influenced me to initially form a negative self-view. We can decide to be actively engaged and focus on the supernatural purpose of our lives. I welcome and am welcomed by those who believe, love, and give.

When choosing to be the best we can be, we can begin by adopting a new perspective. Individuals who have experienced pain often feel bruised to the point where they suffer feelings of apathy and hopelessness. They may have a range of cascading emotions that influence them toward choosing things that are way below their potential.

In the gym, personal trainers are useful because they can see beyond the fatigue a client may feel. If working alone, the client may achieve less in order to feel more comfortable. Personally, it had been over six months since I had trained with a personal trainer and I did not realize how comfortable I had become. During the first circuit trainings that week, I could hardly keep up. It appeared that everyone around me was whizzing by and showing off all of the reps they could do. I almost felt defeated until I reminded myself that this was my best. I could see the pool of perspiration I had produced. I realized that I could keep my focus on the personal goals I set for myself that day.

Often, individuals like me who struggle to maintain a healthy lifestyle may cringe at a setback, but the key is to look beyond the emotions and press forward. To be our best self is the admission that we are using our best effort toward the goals we initially set. We are not comparing our triumphs or pitfalls to the next person by just being sober-minded in approaching our goals.

Questions for Growth:

A. Who were the people who influenced your self-perception as a young person?

B. Why was this positive or negative experience for you?

C. What do you think their best intentions were?

D. How can you reclaim your power from the influence of this experience?

Day Thirty-Seven: Tomorrow Cannot Wait

Breaking Bad Habits

Many adults fail to make true changes because of poor habits. This can be symbolic of a sequence of events where an individual begins to make change and then slowly returns to poor habits. For example, an individual might decide to lose thirty pounds. They eventually take all of the steps: joining the gym, tracking weight loss, starting a blog, and even buying protein shakes between workouts.

At the start, they will probably see some results. Having seen this, they may add one snack to their daily regime and, as time continues, realize that they have slowly allowed poor eating habits back into their diet. Indeed, this is something I have struggled with. I lost over thirty pounds. But now I'm at a place where I crave the things I walked away from.

What is it that makes us abandon our dreams, goals, and desires? Truly, we have to become our own master teachers and healers. I'm not saying we don't need our certified health and therapeutic professionals. But our answer also lies between moments of diagnosis and treatment. We still have our thoughts, relationships, and inner communication to contend with. No one understands your heart the way you do. No one can really tap into your dreams the way you can. Ideally, you can commit to a new level of personal life success but also raise your awareness in the areas in which you would like to improve.

The subject of my doctoral research was the persistence of adult learners. One measure of persistence is the level of dedication a person gives to a particular cause. All too often, we are weakest in areas where we have devoted the least attention. It is easier to blame others for influencing our lives in a poor manner.

We must resolve again to adopt our inner selves. The little child within each person desires the love, admiration, validation, and peace that were needed when we were small. Consider making a vow to live a new life.

Questions for Growth:

A. What is one habit you are trying to break?
B. What are your feelings about you inability to conquer this area of your life?
C. Consider locating one or two people from your support network who can keep you accountable toward making stronger improvements in this area.

Day Thirty-Eight: Tomorrow Can't Wait

Making a Vow!

One of the best days of my life was when I married my hubby, Manuel Da Graca. Hubby was a true blessing. He was smart, multilingual, globalized, well-versed, and open to challenges. He was unique, canny, and fun. He is a man I like to call Eskimo eyes, with a mahogany rouge skin tone.

I was so excited on the day he proposed. I found that not only did I anticipate the actual wedding day, I was excited that we would be able to explore so many of our perspectives and challenges together.

Nothing could adequately describe our wedding day. While not lavish, the love of our friends and family made it very special. Beyond the dress and the wedding ritual, I can especially remember the attentiveness and reminders to remain calm and focused. I heard everything from "This is your day" to "Remember to think positive thoughts." Some in the planning crew assured me that even if some of the guests were problematic, they would do everything to make sure I was comfortable. Others reminded me to get ample rest and to experience full joy and contentment. I completely absorbed the feedback and had a fabulous day. After it was over, I couldn't even remember who was at the wedding until I watched the video. I was truly in the moment.

Wow! What would life be like if we lived this way daily? Maybe this is where the true challenge lies. Since we don't usually have a large event like this to anticipate, we struggle to maintain positive attitudes, block poor thinking, and find ourselves living less effectively than we could. Try to create a fresh outlook on your life and proactively decide to limit anything that may rob you of the peace you so desperately need.

Questions for Growth:

A. On a scale of 1–10, how would you describe the level of peace you have on a daily basis?
B. Which experiences or moments in the week cause the most stress for you?
C. What steps can you take to limit interaction with negative people in an effort to maintain higher levels of peace?

Day Thirty-Nine: Tomorrow Can't Wait

Be Willing to Grow

As a person who helps others, I receive many phone calls from people seeking advice on their relationships and more. More often than not, a person will call me to say they *need* to talk, and then spend about an hour explaining their situation. The rapidity of their voice tells me they want the pain to stop immediately. They lack control to cope with their emotions. In response, I have to carefully gauge the discussion to find out how I can help this person move from one place of unfulfillment to a brighter future. Truly, it can be challenging.

For example, one person called to discuss the pain of a broken heart. Interestingly, they seemed to be using self-blame to control the outcome. This is also typical for cases where domestic violence has occurred. When we have to react to someone who has treated us poorly, we need to examine their persistent behaviors. This is a guide to the history and character of a person. The pain that we receive from others can be devastating.

Once, when I was looking over my personal journal, I noticed that I had cried enough tears to fill the Charles River. I felt drained, as if I had no more tears to offer. As I reflected on the pain I had absorbed and internalized, I came to a point that felt like desperation.

A counselor who occasionally helped me with my own life challenges once asked me to write a list of things for which I was holding people accountable. Boy, I had so many! I was upset about my vulnerability in absorbing hurtful messages from people. There were many times I harbored negative words that pierced me so deeply. I absorbed all of the messages that media had told me about womanhood and beauty. Although I fought against these words, I still was baffled by the discrepancies of society as a whole. I realized that I truly was angry. I was holding the memories and actions of others inside myself and blaming them.

In my talk with the counselor, we channeled my levels of unforgiveness. I was getting angrier the more I continued to talk about my disdain for those who mistreated, lied, made fun of, and accused me. She asked me to have compassion for them. That made me even more upset, for I felt that the last thing they deserved was my compassion.

Revictimization occurs when someone successfully expresses their pain but the person listening to them belittles the hurtful experience. They may tell you the wound just wasn't important.

Oh, how little we understand. No one clearly understands the Post Traumatic Stress Disorder (PTSD) of a war victim. No one can understand the pain of an individual who lost loved ones in an earthquake. No one can completely understand the pain of surviving 9/11. People may not have gone through experiences to this extent, but pain is one common denominator of every hurtful experience.

Painful experiences originate with varying sequences of events. For many years, I held onto resentment, anger, and shame from instances of hurt I endured over the years. While this did not help me move toward a brighter future, it changed when I decided to wake up and smell the roses. I learned to accept fresh rays of sunlight on a daily basis. It was a gift when I finally became ready to let go. While I'm not fully at a place of perfection now, I am well beyond the place of stagnancy where I was years ago.

Joyfully, I learned to accept these pains and begin to perceive them as gifts.

Questions for Growth:

A. What are some areas of growth you have had since you began this journey?

B. Jot down the individuals you still hold accountable for influencing you in a negative way.

C. Consider locating one or two books about forgiveness that can help you move forward.

Day Forty: Tomorrow Can't Wait

Stillness:
The Ability to Just *Be*

For the last couple of weeks, I have been enjoying awesome moments of awareness. Still moved by the challenge of being still, I decided to research the sycamore tree. Amazingly, the sycamore bears figs that offer nourishment to ants, wasps, bees, monkeys, birds, and more. This tree originates in eastern areas of Africa. While watching the PBS documentary entitled *The Queen of Trees*, I was amazed at how much life this tree is able to extend.

As an amateur botanist, I knew that nature had its benefits, but I had no idea how intricate the biology of this tree was. The sap produced from its bark is nourished by ants. A number of parasites and wasps must enter the fig in order to bring forth additional life. Interestingly, too, the seeds of the sycamore tree cannot be replanted at the base. Instead, for new planting, they must be transported by bats, monkeys, fish, or water. This tree also has random seasonal periods that make it useful for the animals and insects it serves.

While mesmerized by intricate images in the PBS documentary, I could not help but compare this documentary to life itself. The sycamore tree looks to the sun to make enough sugar to begin the process of producing figs. Similarly, when we want to move forward in life, we have to not only face our challenges but also look above our situations for enlightenment and awareness of solutions.

Amazingly, all of the insects and animals that feed on the sycamore tree work in a special rhythm. Bees have to bypass ants to begin the honey production process. Monkeys have to eat figs but also watch out so they won't be stung by the bees. Bats come at night to fetch a fig and transport it elsewhere.

Comparing this to human life, I realized that negative experiences and people can be like the wasps that nest in the sycamore. They are never pleasant, but they can serve a valuable purpose. Although we see them as a pestilence, they nurture us and add to the development of life. As I reflected on this, I was reminded of the wisdom and gratitude I learned as a result of experiencing failure, loss, and pain.

It always reminds me of the question students and professionals ask: "Dr. D, you have so much energy. Where does it come from?"

I usually reply that it's not that I haven't experienced difficult moments. Believe me, I've had many. It's not that I never struggled, because I remember the challenge of struggling to pay for college on a weekly basis. I can recall trying to keep focused amid the temptations of the freedoms young people are exposed to.

I also remember the day I questioned whether my life was worth living. I struggled for my own self-acceptance. My perspective of life came down to the questions, Why does life seem so difficult? Why can't I feel okay? What does this all mean?

Later, ten years from that time, I walked into a Jamaica Plain, Massachusetts, bookstore and discovered my first self-help book. If I hadn't been led to do that,

I'm not sure I would be at this place in my life today. Naturally, I had listened to my mentors, attended church, gone to women's seminars, and learned lessons from my experiences of serving others that steered me back in the right direction. In the midst of hardships, I made a vow that I would always tell my truth. This desire has given me a passion to coach and guide individuals like those of you who are reading this book. My hope is that you pull this book out time and time again.

Do not be afraid to seek professional counsel from individuals who have the knowledge and expertise to assist you in moving forward. Feel free to participate in the online workshops, seminars, and meetings that I will offer from my coaching and educational services. The thought of seeking help can be annoying, like the wasp is to the monkey trying to grab a fig to eat from the sycamore tree. It comes with a price of time and dedication that may appear like a waste of time. But, like the sycamore tree, if we confront and pay attention to our challenges, we may experience a blooming season—a new stage of discovery that we may have never encountered! Keep moving forward!

Sitting outside with the trees, I see there's so much action happening under a boring tree. It seems like nothing is happening, but everything is happening.

Questions to Consider:

A. What has been your greatest aspect of learning since participating in this forty-day guide?

B. What are some new discoveries you have found about yourself?

C. Consider making an action plan that lists the steps you will take in the next three months to continue your spiritual growth and introspection.

About the Author

Dr. Allana Todman-Da Graca, is a Mass Communications Specialist who teaches adult learners within the online learning environment. She holds a Doctorate in Education, and a Master's in New Media. Dr. Todman-Da Graca has developed a passion for helping all learners persist in their personal and professional lives. She has a keen interest in helping women and teen girls to develop the courage and tenacity to become effective in their varying spheres of influence. She has published a book of poetry which is entitled, Temple: Self Discovery Through Truth.